Jerry Rumple

D0559213

Let's Build an Evangelistic Church

By Dr. Jack Hyles

SWORD OF THE LORD PUBLISHERS
Box 1099, Murfreesboro, Tennessee

Copyright 1962 by
SWORD OF THE LORD PUBLISHERS

ISBN 0-87398-502-8

Printed in U.S.A.

Table of Contents

Introduction

Do you know Jack Hyles? Do you know the man who is pastor of the First Baptist Church of Hammond, Indiana, and president of Baptist Bible College of Denver, Colorado? I believe that you will know him after you read this vital and interesting book.

I have just gone through the manuscript of Dr. Hyle's book, *Let's Build an Evangelistic Church*. A score of adjectives kept flashing through my mind as I read the pages — "practical," "sympathetic," "humorous," "convicting," "understandable," etc. Such words will come before you as you read. Here is a book that touches many vital subjects in a minister's life: personal soul winning, visitation, church invitations, time schedules for busy pastors, the pastor and his family.

This is the book for the busy pastor. Here are ways to increase efficiency in use of time. Here is a book for the man who has had mediocre success in the ministry, but has the desire to do more for the glory of God. This is a book for the pastor who has failed. Failure brings discouragement, fears, despondency.

Let me suggest something to all pastors and Christian workers — READ THIS BOOK! It will revitalize your ministry. It will bless your home. It will stir your church.

LEE ROBERSON, Pastor
Highland Park Baptist Church
Chattanooga, Tennessee

May 21, 1962

Foreword

As a young preacher starting out many years ago, I read the Book of Acts over and over again. I went to my knees and asked God to let me have a ministry and build churches that would be akin to the Book of Acts. When this was settled before God, my little country church in East Texas became a hotbed of soul winning, even though we were ten miles out in the country. God gave us souls every week and a perennial revival spirit. The methods we used there were basically the methods presented in this book.

For seven years we labored in the Miller Road Baptist Church, Garland, Texas. Using these methods, the Lord led us and used our people to grow a church from 44 members to 4,128 members in six and a half years.

I am doing my best now as pastor of the First Baptist Church of Hammond, Indiana, to lead our people to this kind of a Book of Acts ministry. "They that were scattered abroad went everywhere preaching the Word."

While in West Palm Beach, Florida, in a Bible Conference with Dr. John R. Rice approximately five years ago, my attention was called to the parable of the Great Supper in Luke 14:16-23. I resolved to go home to my church and plan my church program according to the commandments in this parable. You will notice in this parable we are commanded to go into the streets, and the lanes, to bring in the lame, the poor, the halt, and the blind, and to go into the highways and hedges. We have organized our church literally according to this parable. For two weeks our people did exactly what the parable says.

The word "streets" seems to mean city streets. Forty of our men spent every hour they had off from work on the main streets of Dallas, Texas, witnessing, passing out tracts, spreading the Gospel. This was done day and night.

The word "lanes" seems to mean small streets. Four hundred and thirty-eight people went from house to house in the city of Garland telling everybody how to be saved. When we left Garland, Texas, in 1959, we had the assurance that our church had knocked on every door in the city of Garland. Perhaps some were missed, but we do not know of them. Our people literally went from house to house in the lanes of our city for two weeks.

Notice it says, "Bring in hither the poor," in the parable of the Great Supper. This we also did. We organized teams to go into poor sections of our town and visit house to house every poor family we could find. Many of these poor people were reached with the Gospel of Christ.

Also the parable says, "Bring in the maimed, the halt, and the blind." Ten of our ladies spent two weeks every day going into the hospitals of our city visiting the maimed, the halt, and the blind. Every sick person in every hospital in our town was visited by our membership.

Again, the Lord commands us to go into the highways. We organized a team of forty men to witness on every highway leading out of our city. They stopped at every house, every business place, every service station, every tavern, between our town and the next towns and witnessed on the highways.

The last commandment is that we go to the hedges. We took this to mean the country roads and rural areas. Ten of our ladies volunteered to spend two weeks going out the country roads and visiting every farm home and every rural house between our town and the next town on every country road. Our young people also went out in the rural areas and conducted street services with loudspeakers.

On the opening Sunday of this two-week period, our church authorized me to baptize anyone at any time. This I did. We filled the baptistry and kept it filled for two weeks. People would call me in the middle of the night and say, "Preacher, I just won a soul. He wants to get baptized." I would get out of bed, go to the church, and baptize the convert. We baptized every day for two weeks.

When the two weeks ended, over five hundred people were scattered all over the town and area witnessing for Christ. Thirty-eight of our young people had spent practically day and night on the public square of our city passing out tracts and witnessing. Over sixty were won to Christ by the young people alone. Three hundred thirty-three people were saved in this two-week period. Over one hundred and twenty-five people won someone to Christ. One lady won seventeen to Christ. One man won seventeen to Christ. We had baptized scores of people. Our attendance increased, and the spirit of our church must have been the spirit of those in the Book of Acts who were scattered abroad everywhere preaching the Word.

From that beginning comes this book. We have made no attempt to be scholarly, but a definite attempt to be practical. The first work done on the book was done on a train between Dallas, Texas, and Washington, D. C. One chapter was outlined in the wee hours of the morning waiting for a plane at Stapleton Airport in Denver, Colorado. One chapter was outlined on a jet plane between Chicago and New York City. Work has been done in depots, airports, on trains, planes, at home at night, and other places, to make this a manual for those who want to be soul winners. May God use it in the building of churches who will "live in the Book of Acts."

JACK HYLES,
Hammond, Indiana

1
Let's Build a Visitation Program

In reading the Book of Acts, one of the most impressive things we find is that the New Testament Christians were scattered abroad everywhere preaching the Word. Nearly two thousand years since this atmosphere, we find the most pressing problem in the church — that of visitation. All across the country pastors ask me, "How can we get people to visit? How can we get folks on the field? How do you reach people?"

While not pretending to know all the answers or even most of the answers, we hope in this chapter to leave a few suggestions and ideas that will be helpful to pastors and churches across the country.

1. Become Known As An Evangelistic Center

This is of utmost importance in the growing of an evangelistic church. If a church could become *the* evangelistic church in a town, and a pastor could become *the* evangelistic pastor in a town, people would call on him and call on the church in an effort to get their loved ones saved. The world, whether we like it or not, looks at churches as specialists. The world looks upon one church as a certain type, another

church as another type. I always want my church to be known
as the evangelistic-type church.

For example, recently a lady called and asked me to visit
her brother who was dying in the hospital. I asked her if she
were a Christian. She answered yes, she was. I asked if she
had a pastor. She answered yes. I asked her why she did not
ask her pastor to go. "Oh," she replied, "my pastor doesn't
specialize in those cases."

Needless to say, I try to specialize in those cases myself.
So I went to the hospital and led her brother to the Lord.
He passed away a few days later.

The church should make a big enough racket about soul
winning and evangelism that people from far and wide will
know it is an evangelistic church.

Sometimes people who have lost loved ones will bring the
lost loved ones to such a church to be saved, then take them
back to their own church to be baptized and to serve. This is
because they know that a particular church is the best place
for evangelism in an area. This is an important thing in
building a visitation program.

2. The Pastor Should Visit Constantly Himself

A pastor who is not active in visitation will not lead his
people to be active in visitation. The pastor who does not
visit regularly will not train people to visit regularly. When
the pastor is leading folks to Christ regularly and week after
week new Christians are walking the aisles whom the pastor
has won, then the people will get the idea and follow him.

Remember that a leader is one who does first that which
he expects the followers to do. A good way in the beginning
is to learn the streets in the town. Just as a policeman or a
fireman would learn the streets, even so must the soul
winner. When I accept a new pastorate I usually spend the
first week driving around town learning the streets. The
streets in a town may be learned easily, such as the num-

bered streets — First, Second, Third, etc. Then Avenue A, Avenue B, Avenue C. In some towns the streets in a certain community are named after the states; in some towns they are named after presidents. Usually there is some pattern in the naming of streets. It is important that this pattern be learned.

When you visit, route yourself. Get your prospect cards, divide them according to sections of town, and make a regular route. Usually I take the same route every day, thereby enabling more visits to be made.

Some people seem to think that they hire the preacher to do the visiting. Some preachers seem to think that it is their job to preach and the people are to do the visiting. Both are wrong. Both pastor and people together should be reaching people for Christ and should actively participate in the visitation program.

3. Every Service Should Be An Evangelistic Service

To be sure, every sermon cannot be a sermon just to win the lost. There must be sermons on consecration, dedication, stewardship, faithfulness, etc. But every service should have an evangelistic appeal, with an invitation for sinners to be saved. It is the pastor's job to be certain that each service is evangelistic, thereby not disappointing his people who bring their lost loved ones and friends. Many times church members will bring a lost loved one or friend to the services, and the pastor does not give a strong evangelistic appeal. This discourages the members from bringing lost loved ones and discourages visitation.

In our churches we have tried constantly to make every service a service where it is easy to be saved. If we preach on comfort, we close with the thought that the best comfort is to know that you are saved, that you know you would go to Heaven if you died. If we preach on stewardship, we close by reminding the people that the greatest gift we can give to the Lord is the gift of our lives, and the greatest gift that He has ever given is the gift of His Son and salvation through His Son. If we preach on consecration, we remind our audience in closing that there can be no consecration until there has been regeneration. Regardless of the sermon or the type of service, there can be an evangelistic emphasis, with a pungent invitation to sinners which will keep the people bringing lost ones to the services.

One of our ladies called recently to say, "Brother Hyles, I am bringing a lost loved one to church next Sunday morning, and I just wanted to tell you about it. . . . Oh, all of our services are evangelistic now, aren't they? Praise the Lord, I can bring my lost loved ones anytime and be sure that you will try to get them saved."

4. Make Soul Winning Dwarf Everything Else That Goes on in the Church

In other words, make soul winning the most important phase of the church program. Far too many people think that being a deacon or a Sunday School teacher is the biggest job in the church. Our people should constantly be reminded that the greatest job in the New Testament church is bringing people to Jesus Christ. If we as pastors will magnify the job of soul winning above any other job in the church, then the people will get the idea that being a soul winner is the greatest position that they can hold.

5. Do Not Train a Church of Specialists

As I see the condition of many of our churches, we have taught our people, perhaps subconsciously but at least we have left the impression, that each person has a job to do in the church. Some do soul winning; some have other tasks. This is certainly a detrimental thing. Every Christian is commanded to be a soul winner; soul winning is every Christian's job. For a person to think that operating the business of the church is his particular special field and that is all, is wrong. For a person to think that his job is teaching the Bible alone is also wrong. Every Christian's job is soul winning. Every phase of our church life must be permeated with this atmosphere, and every leader of our church should be reminded that the main job is bringing sinners to Christ.

Someone said to Mr. Moody one time when witnessed to by him, "Tend to your own business."

Mr. Moody said, "Soul winning is my business, sir."

6. Create An Evangelistic Atmosphere in the Church Services

To a great extent, evangelism is more an atmosphere than anything else. If we want a revival-type service every Sunday, then we must try to create a revival-type atmosphere every Sunday. This would include revival-type music, revival-type testimonies, revival-type preaching, revival-type invitations, etc. Perhaps the results on Sunday have more to do with the atmosphere of the service than any of us realize. If we have high church-type music, a ritualistic order of service, an ultra-formal message, and a high church atmosphere, how can we expect evangelistic results. It is so important that the atmosphere of our churches and of our services be conducive to a perennial harvest of souls.

7. Have Periodic Soul Winning Instruction Classes

At least once a year, and maybe more often, we have soul-winning courses in our church. This is a very simple course, much like the one found in this book on how to lead a soul to Christ.

Sometimes this course is taught for three consecutive nights; for example, Monday, Tuesday, Wednesday; or

Thursday, Friday, Saturday; or Wednesday, Thursday, Friday. Sometimes it is taught on Wednesday nights for a period of four to six weeks. Our most recent course was of this nature — five consecutive Wednesday nights given to the learning of how to win a soul to Christ.

8.   There Should Be a Definite Time for Visitation

Most churches have a definite night for visitation. Some use Monday night, some Tuesday, some Thursday, some even Friday. It has long been our conviction that Monday and Thursday are the best nights for visitation since this makes it closer to the Sunday and Wednesday night services and makes it easier to promote attendance. You can get promises on Sunday night and Wednesday night from those who will come and pretty well determine your attendance by these pledges. We have found it very profitable to use Wednesday night even for visitation. After the service on Wednesday night, and after an emphasis on visitation, ask the people who will promise to make four or five visits that week to raise their hands. Have the visitation secretary or someone with the cards at the door in the back. They can get the cards before they leave and turn them back in before Sunday. This has been especially beneficial in our church in Hammond due to the fact that we are a downtown church and people travel so many miles to our services.

9.   Stress Visitation Constantly and Get Visitation Testimonies and Reports

Each Wednesday evening we ask for a report from our people during the regular midweek service as to how many visits were made the preceding week. We also keep a record of the number of visits made and the number of folks who have witnessed to someone during the week. Also we ask for a report from the folks who have lead someone to Christ during the previous seven days. Then we have testimonies concerning these reports. We are always thrilled to hear the reports and find how many of our people are witnessing week after week.

10. Choose Your Church Leaders From Those Who Visit

No doubt one of the most tragic things in the modern church is that we have turned over the leadership of our church in many cases to unspiritual people who never make a visit. The false assumption that because a person is a successful businessman he can be a successful church leader is decaying the spiritual life of many churches. Because a man is bank president does not mean that he would make a good deacon chairman. Because a man is a civic leader does not mean he is a good church leader.

A man should not be chosen for an office or overlooked for an office because of his position in the neighborhood but because of his spiritual gifts and spiritual life and dedication to Christ. In our churches we have tried to choose Sunday School teachers who visit, deacons who visit, church leaders who visit, trustees who visit, and constantly stress that no person is qualified to be a leader of a church unless he is carrying out the Great Commission of our Saviour. The heart of the New Testament church was soul winning. If that be the case, the heart of the twentieth century church should be soul winning. Hence, the leadership should be composed of those who are visiting and reaching folks for Christ.

11. Give Due Recognition to Soul Winners and Folks Who Visit

Be sure that people who are successful in visitation receive due recognition in the services. This is not to magnify them, but to encourage others and let others know what is being done and what can be done when a person means business for God. When someone wins a soul to Christ and he walks the aisle on Sunday, have the soul winner stand beside the new convert and let them rejoice together. If you know of some soul winners in your church doing an exceptional job, include them in one of your sermons so as to encourage them and others because of the work that is being done in the church. Occasionally bring someone whom you have lead to Christ to the platform. Lead them to Christ and show the people exactly how you did it. Go through it step by step.

Better still, have one of the lay soul winners in the church bring one of their converts to the platform and show how he led him to Christ. This will give the people an eyewitness account and show them what to do rather than tell them.

12. Go With Different People Yourself

One of the best ways in the world to train soul winners is to go visiting with different people if you are an effective soul winner. Let them observe your methods and your tactics. Before long, they can solo themselves and no doubt will become effective soul winners.

This is the method Jesus used. He trained a few well, rather than trying to train a thousand. He trained twelve. They observed and learned by watching. The soul winner may take with him some prospective soul winners. They may observe him and his methods, thereby learning themselves how to win others.

One of the best soul winners I know is Bob Keyes, pastor of the Galilean Baptist Church in Dallas, Texas. Brother Keyes came to work as my assistant pastor many years ago in Garland, Texas. He had never won a soul. For three years he went with me. Week after week, day after day, house to house, he observed and learned. Now he is one of the finest soul winners in America. The same can be said about my assistant pastor at the First Baptist Church in Hammond, Rev. Jim Lyons. He first went with others, saw their methods, then went on his own.

A good idea for a pastor is to let his people know the days that he visits. If any man in the church wants to visit with him the day the pastor visits, let the men know they are welcome. No doubt, observing others doing it is one of the greatest ways to make soul winners.

13. In Each Group of Cards Passed Out on Visitation Night, Place One Good Prospect

If you can guarantee each group going out to visit at least one good visit, it will be a tremendous help. Visitation will become a delight to them rather than a drudgery. We have tried through the years to place at least one good prospect in every group, thereby insuring every one of at least one blessing. This will more than likely encourage them to come back again for the visitation program.

14. Do Not Wear the People Out Doing Other Things

Too much could not be said about this. People who are busy doing other things besides soul winning often will not have enough time to do soul winning. Many of our churches are so highly organized and people are so busy doing little things, they have absolutely no time left for the main thing. A church that is too highly organized will not usually train effective soul winners. A church that keeps the people working on smaller tasks and odds and ends too much will have a difficult time training good personal soul winners. A church that has too much going on and uses too many of the people's nights on other things besides soul winning will have a difficult time training good soul winners.

It is so important that the life in our church, the main

job in our church, the heartbeat of our church, the hub of our church, and every activity of our church be built upon soul winning and reaching people for Jesus Christ. Too many of our people are on a spiritual merry-go-round. They spend all their time going around in circles, get off right where they got on, and get absolutely nowhere.

15. Some Suggestions Concerning the Visitation Service Itself

If the church has visitation on a week night (and most visiting churches do), it is important that the visitation services be conducted properly.

Prior to the service the visitation file should have been observed and cards drawn from the file for visitation. From four to six cards should be placed in a group usually by geographical location. Enough groups of cards to take care of the visitation crowd should be chosen and prepared and brought to the visitation assembly room. It would be good for the pastor and church leaders to get there a few minutes early before the visitation service starts for a time of fellowship, handshaking, chatting, etc. before the visitation actually starts. As the people come, the pastor may compliment the people with a "God bless you, Jim," or, "I'm glad to see you tonight, Joe," or, "Isn't this the first time you have been to visitation, James? What a blessing it is to have you with us." These greetings will mean something to the people.

Then at visitation time a song or two could be sung. A good song to sing is to the tune of "Leaning on the Everlasting Arms":

> Oh, how sweet to walk, round and round the block,
>> Ringing doorbells for my Lord.
> Wearing out my shoes, telling God's Good News,
>> Ringing doorbells for my Lord.
> Ringing, ringing, ringing doorbells for my Lord,
> Wearing out my shoes, telling God's Good News,
>> Ringing doorbells for my Lord.

Or a good one to sing is "Bringing in the Sheaves." Still other good songs to sing would be such songs as "Send the Light," "I Love to Tell the Story," etc.

Then have a few testimonies before going. Have some testify as to what visitation has meant to them. Perhaps they were saved on visitation. Perhaps they have won someone recently. These testimonies would put the people in a spiritual attitude before going.

After this, perhaps the pastor or visitation leader could give a few pointers on visitation, showing how the church could be more effective in its visitation program and perhaps correcting any errors that have been made in past visitation.

Then the people should be divided to go out two by two. Some people already will have partners chosen before the visitation service. Still others must be paired off at the church. People of mutual interest and social standing usually visit better together. The pastor or visitation chairman should be very careful in pairing the people off. It is always good for an inexperienced and an experienced visitor to go together. The pastor should encourage more experienced soul winners to take inexperienced partners so as to train them in the art of visitation and soul winning.

After the people have been paired off in twos, then the cards may be passed out. It is a good idea to have a brief prayer before going. Ask each person to pray for the people they will visit by name. They may go through the cards. After this prayer, leave in an orderly manner and make the visits.

16. Visitation Programs Must Vary and Change

We have found that a certain type visitation program will work effectively for a certain amount of time. Then another should be inaugurated with a big push. This eliminates over-stressing every week the visitation program. It should not be stressed to the same extent each week, else the people become so accustomed to hearing it that they scarcely hear what is said.

For example, we have found it wise to change the night periodically. Visit for a year on Monday night, then try Thursday, then maybe Tuesday. New thoughts and ideas should constantly be presented with a big push and a church-wide emphasis.

Bear in mind, it is the same old thing of going after sinners, but with a new thought, a new stress, a new idea, a new way of promoting.

17.   Use Busses, Bus Drivers, and Bus Captains

One of the most effective ways in reaching people with the Gospel of Christ is by using properly the bus ministry. Presently, in the First Baptist Church in Hammond, we are operating ten bus routes. Just this morning before dictating this chapter my assistant pastor and I decided to add a new bus route within a matter of days, making a total of eleven. Let us notice a few thoughts about the busses.

A few busses could be owned by the church. Our church presently owns six busses. Bear in mind, we have eleven bus routes, which means we have to secure five busses elsewhere. The reason we own any busses at all is not only for Sunday School and church routes, but also for youth programs, rescue mission activities, etc. Our young people go to camp each year on the busses, and they are certainly a valuable asset. Even the smallest church could own one bus and find it a real help.

Busses may be rented or leased. In many cities, the City Transit Company would rent busses at a fair price. In some cities, a bus can be rented from a school or another agency. At the present time we are renting five buses very inexpensively to supplement the six that we own.

Find consecrated bus captains. After preaching some sermons about the bus ministry, and bringing constant challenges before the people about the bus ministry, God has laid it upon the heart of twenty to twenty-five of our people to dedicate their lives to the ministry of bringing people on the busses.

For example, we usually choose two captains for each bus. We simply give them a bus and let them fill it up. Two of our ladies got burdened about the bus ministry. They asked for a bus, and we provided one for them. They went to a government housing project and within six weeks they had filled the bus with over forty people. They came to us and asked for another bus. Now they are filling two busses every week with over sixty people who were not being reached a few months ago.

Two of our ladies were burdened about a neighboring city. We told them that they could have a bus if they would fill it up. They went to the neighboring city, started going from house to house, and in a matter of ten weeks have filled the bus. Just this morning they asked for another bus for their city.

Two of our choir members got burdened about a certain area in our city. They asked for a bus. The first week they made over two hundred visits and have averaged over one hundred and fifty visits per week for the last five weeks. Needless to say, they are rapidly filling their bus.

Two of our deacons asked for a bus. Within ten weeks they filled two busses and now are bringing in nearly one hundred every Sunday. These are people who were not being reached before these deacons got burdened.

Route the busses by areas of town. When we start a bus route, we first get two captains and make several suggestions as to an area. We feel that an area of two to four square miles, or less if possible, is sufficient area for a good bus route. We ask the captains to pray about three or four different areas, choosing the one they feel impressed to work. Once they choose the area, it is their job to visit the absentees just like a Sunday School class and to go house to house trying to find people to ride the busses.

Have a weekly meeting with the bus pastors. This meeting is simply to stimulate interest, get reports and plans, inspire, work, etc.

Give special recognition to successful bus pastors in the public services. Let the people know what is going on and constantly keep the bus ministry before the people.

If possible, secure drivers for the busses apart from the bus captains. This will put more people to work. For example, we will be operating eleven busses soon. If there are eleven bus drivers, twenty-two bus captains, then there are thirty-three people working on the busses. This puts more people to work and is a pretty good crew in itself.

Contests between busses. One of the finest ways to increase attendance is to have a contest between busses and bus routes. A simple award may be given at the end of the contest to the team members of the winning bus. Over three hundred people per Sunday are now riding busses to the First Baptist Church of Hammond. People are saved every Sunday who ride the busses. A well-organized, spiritually-planned bus ministry could put new life into many churches.

18. Teach the Young Christians to Bring Their Lost Friends

A young Christian perhaps could not win a soul adeptly. However, he does know perhaps more lost people than the pastor knows. Even as the woman in John 4 went back to the city and told those with whom she had sinned about Jesus and brought them to hear Him, so we encourage our converts to bring people to hear the preacher and the Gospel.

19. Start Folks Visiting Absentees

You may get the folks in the habit of visiting by getting

the people to start visiting absentees. Give them some easy ones at first. They could be people who have been out sick a week or two. Give them some folks to visit in the hospital. Get them in the habit of visiting. After a while they will be able to take a little harder case and still harder, until finally they can be sent out to win souls themselves.

It was many years after I began visiting before I became a proficient soul winner. A person must get the feel of visitation. This can be done by encouraging people to visit hospitals, absentees, etc.

20.   Occasionally Have Skits

Perhaps someone whom you have won to Christ recently could be brought to the platform and that experience could be relived to the advantage of the people. They could actually see you win the person. Use the same conversation that you used in the home, the same Scriptures, etc. Just win the person again, so to speak, so the people can see how it is done. This is tremendously important.

21.   Through It All, Build An Old-Fashioned, Sin-Hating, Christ-Honoring, Soul-Winning, Bible-Preaching Church

Let the people know every Sunday that you are for old-fashioned soul winning. Encourage the people to say "Amen" to the preacher. It is important that the atmosphere of the service be akin to the New Testament atmosphere. We encourage our people to say "Amen." We encourage them to participate in the services. We sing gospel music at every service. The people know that we are preaching to get results and have people saved.

Every preacher should have to watch a jewelry auctioneer in action at least once in his life. Several years ago Mrs. Hyles and I were in Hot Springs, Arkansas, for a vacation. We were captivated by the jewelry auctions in the jewelry stores across from Bathhouse Row in Hot Springs. One night I suggested to the wife that we go sit in the back at one of the auctions and watch the "suckers" buy the merchandise. We had an agreement before going that we would say nothing. We planned to sit on the back row, not participate in the auction at all, say nothing, smile at nothing, and just watch the people bite.

The auctioneer stood and sold a travel iron for two or three dollars. Mrs. Hyles said, "We should have bought that. That was a steal."

I said, "Hush. We came to watch, not to buy."

Then he sold a beautiful waffle iron for about five dollars. Mrs. Hyles looked at me and said, "Honey, I could have used that."

I said, "Be quiet. We did not come to buy, we came to watch."

Several other things were auctioned. We did not make a single bid or a single move to show our interest.

Suddenly the auctioneer cried with a loud voice, "How many folks are here from Texas?" Before we realized it, our hands were up, and we were happily admitting we were Texans. He asked what town we were from. We told him. He said, "Why don't you Texans move down to the front." We had no choice. We moved to the front.

Several hours later we left the auction. Mrs. Hyles had a diamond ring on her finger. I had a travel iron and two or three other objects. We had spent $52 of the $58 we had left of our vacation money and had to go home two days early!

The moral is this: Everything in that meeting was geared to results. The opening, the friendliness, the stories, the handshaking, the asking of "Where are you from?" the intense interest, the salesmanship of the auctioneer — everything was geared for one thing, to sell the merchandise.

The church of the Lord Jesus Christ should be geared for one thing, and that is to bring people to Jesus. Every song we sing should point toward that. All of our church life should be built around the reaching of people for Jesus Christ.

To be sure, we must occasionally have stewardship emphasis. But the reason we have stewardship emphasis is that people give to spread the Gospel. To be sure, we sing praises to God. But we sing praises to God out of appreciation for salvation and for the fact that we are able to win others to His Son. To be sure, we must teach consecration and faithfulness. And yet all of it must have a major underlying emphasis, and that is that people are dying without Christ and are going to Hell forever.

May we diligently give ourselves to this, the greatest task in all the world.

2
Let's Find the Prospects

One of the biggest problems that all soul-winning churches face is that of finding sufficient prospects to visit. This is especially true in a small town or rural area, but this problem can be alleviated.

The pastor should constantly be after his people to turn in prospects. Unsaved people are like fish. They run in schools. When you get a man converted he knows many, many others who could be reached with the Gospel. Perhaps our best method of obtaining prospects has been to constantly keep before our people the importance of turning names in to us that they feel could be reached for Jesus. These are never what we call "Cold trails." These are people who are being prayed for and will have been bathed in prayer before our visit. Again and again it should be emphasized to the people to turn in prospects to the pastor or the church office.

Those who visit the services. The week after a visitor attends a service he should be called upon by a member of the church staff, preferably by the pastor. This is urgent and should not be overlooked. These are people who know your church and will be your best prospects. They are people who have been in the service, they have felt the breath of Heaven and the presence of the Holy Spirit. They know about the church service and have been blessed by it. These by all means should be visited immediately after their visit.

New-Move List. A new-move list may be obtained in most towns from the Chamber of Commerce, the Retail Merchants Association or utility companies. Very definitely these people should be visited. We have made it a practice through the years to get this list, to send a letter to all the new people in town, inviting them to the church and sending a brochure concerning the advantages the church offers. This should be followed up very shortly by a visit from the church.

Employ a church visitor. This could be a volunteer worker but, if possible, it should be a full-time job. Why not employ a poised, likeable person to be constantly taking a census in the neighborhood; constantly visiting the new people who move to town; getting information concerning their status spiritually, their church preference, etc. From this visit prospect cards can be made and given to the teachers for a visit later. Smaller churches could employ a combination secretary-visitor. Perhaps a lady would work in the church office in the mornings and visit in the afternoons.

Census. Of course, the census is the most used and best way to obtain prospects. This method is simply getting the members together and going from house-to-house canvassing a certain neighborhood for prospects, making prospect cards of each person who is unchurched and giving it to the teacher to visit.

An inside census. We have found this very profitable in rural areas and areas where prospects are limited. An inside church census is simply taking a census of every house where the church members live. Many of the people who attend our churches have unsaved loved ones, unsaved tenants, unsaved

landlords, etc. The inside church census is simply a census of all the families in the church and everyone who lives under their roof. You would be surprised how many prospects can be found in this type of census.

Years ago when I was pastor in the country we took a census and found only seven prospects. Then we took an inside church census and found over a hundred. From these hundred prospects, over forty were saved in a ten-day revival campaign.

3
Let's Go Soul Winning

"Go ye therefore, and teach all nations [Mark's version says, ". . . preach the gospel to every creature"], baptizing them in the name of the Father, and of the Son, and of the Holy Ghost: Teaching them to observe all things whatsoever I have commanded you: and, lo, I am with you alway, even unto the end of the world." — Matt. 28:19, 20.

Notice the simplicity of the Great Commission. I'm satisfied that this is not all it teaches, but this is the basic teaching, as I see it, of the Great Commission. There are several verbs in this verse. The first one is, "*Go.*" We are to go. That means to go where they are. It doesn't mean to put up a shingle in your office and say, "If anybody wants to get saved, inquire within." It means you are to look them up, track them down. You are to go where they are.

The second verb is, "*Teach*" (Mark says, "Preach"). Actually it means to win them. Go out and tell them how to be saved. The first thing you do is to go; then get them saved.

The next verb is, "*Baptize.*"

And then, ". . . Teaching them to observe all things whatsoever I have commanded you."

Notice there are four basic verbs: (1) *Go.* (2) *Preach* (or teach, get them saved). (3) *Baptize.* (4) *Teach* them again.

You teach them something after you get them saved and baptized. What do you teach them? To "... observe all things whatsoever I have commanded you." It did not say to teach "whatsoever I have written you." But teach them "whatsoever I have *commanded* you."

Now what did He command us to do? Go, preach, baptize, then teach them what He commanded us to do. So, we teach them to go and preach and baptize, that they may teach their converts to go, preach and baptize, that they may teach their converts to go and preach and baptize. If I understand the Great Commission properly, the first thing to teach somebody you win to Christ is how to win somebody else to Christ. Don't you think so? It says 'to teach them to do what I have told you to do, what I have commanded you to do.'

Here is what I think the Great Commission basically teaches. I come to this brother here on the front. First, I go. I go to your house; I go to your store, then I tell you how to get converted. I get you baptized. Then I must teach you how to go and get the next man converted and get him baptized, that he may teach another how to go and get still another converted and baptized, that he may go, etc.

Dr. Rice, you don't quit there. You teach him how to get this man converted and baptize him. It is a long circle when you get somebody converted. We have the idea that the Great Commission is wrapped up in going, preaching, and baptizing, and that that is all it says. No, it says you teach them how to go. You teach them how to get folks saved. You teach them how to get folks baptized. That is also a part of the Great Commission and the first command to us after we win a soul to Jesus Christ.

So, this is the Great Commission, this matter of what I'm doing today. I'm teaching you how to have pretty feet. The Bible says, "How beautiful are the feet of them that preach the gospel of peace, and bring glad tidings of good things!" So, I'm a chiropodist, a foot specialist. I'm going to make you have pretty feet. A secret of success is good feet. An athlete will tell you the first things that will go bad are legs and feet. No matter how hard you can bat, how good you can catch and pitch, when your legs are gone, the athlete is gone.

The most important thing about an army is its feet. When I was in the service they had foot inspection at midnight. We would be sound asleep and then ... "Attention!!!" Here comes the Captain. We would stand up and look, and here was that big old boy coming down the hall. They would say, "Get on your foot lockers." We got on our foot lockers. Great big old feet sticking out, and they say, "O.K. Hold up your trousers." We held up our trousers while they examined our feet. Why? Because the most important thing about the army was the feet.

Now the first thing to get cold about you is your feet — physically or spiritually. I was in Phoenix in a conference. I got cold at night and I didn't know I was cold. I wasn't awake enough to know where I was cold, but I was awake enough to know I was cold somewhere. Invariably it is your feet that get cold, but you don't realize it. You start pulling the cover up around your shoulders while your feet are sticking out completely. Your feet get colder and you feel colder, but you don't know where you are cold. You pull the covers a little further. Finally, you are freezing to death. It is your feet that are cold but you don't know it.

And that is the first thing that will get cold spiritually. You start tithing and giving more money. But it is not your pocketbook that is cold; it is your feet. You promise God you will start coming to prayer meeting, but your feet get cold first. And a lot of Christians are as cold as a wedge and don't know where it started. It started with their feet.

The same is true about being dirty. How many of you men (now you ladies wouldn't dare do this, but we men do it quite a bit); you don't want to take a bath. You are not quite dirty enough to take a bath, but your feet are dirty, so you take your shoes off, put your big feet up in the lavatory and wash them. Why? Because the feet get dirty first.

The same is true with a Christian. When the feet get dirty—they are the first things that lead you toward backsliding. The first thing you leave off when you get away from God is not the Sunday School on Sunday morning; it is not the Sunday evening service. The first thing is visitation, calling, witnessing. If you can keep your feet warm, you will be warm all over. If you can keep your feet clean, you will be clean all over. If you can keep your feet right, you will be right all over. So, today we will discuss how to keep your feet pretty.

Soul winning is the basic secret of every other problem in the church. For example, here a church is having cold services. There is no warmth there. The Lord does not meet with them. Now how do you overcome it? Get to winning souls. If somebody walks down the aisle every Sunday and professes their faith in Christ, that will warm the service up a great deal.

Here is a church having trouble with its business. It doesn't have enough folks who know business. It is having trouble handling its legal affairs. It doesn't have enough wisdom. The Bible says, "He that winneth souls is wise." So God gives extra wisdom to those who win souls. I would rather have a soul-winning ignoramous run the business of my church than a group of big shots who won't come to prayer meeting on Wednesday night. In the First Baptist Church in Hammond our deacons and leaders are men not necessarily who are business wise, but men who are spiritual and soul winners because God gives them wisdom that no one else has.

The same is true about your finances. If you have trouble raising your money, just get some sinners converted. When Jesus wanted some money, what did He do? He caught a fish with money in its mouth. The same is true if you will get busy about soul winning. Now if you have a little trouble in the church, go soul winning.

Suppose Dr. Rice and I have a fuss. The best thing for us to do is to go soul winning together. If we can win somebody to Jesus together, we will make it all right. We will love each other again.

When I was in Texas a deacon there had a fuss with me. Of course I thought it was his fault. So, one night he came to visitation. We went visiting together. He said, "Preacher, that Bible study you brought last night was the most ridiculous thing I have ever heard."

I said, "J. B., if you had an ounce of sense, if God gave you a brain the size of a flea's brain, you would know I taught the truth last night."

Now, he said, "Preacher, if I didn't love you, I would quit coming to this church."

I said, "J. B., the truth is, I ought not to even go with you." Boy, we really had it.

About that time we came to the first house. A fellow came to the door in his bathrobe and house slippers. He had gone to bed. We got him converted, and J. B. got happy and we started rejoicing. The fellow woke his wife and she came and got converted. We walked out the door on the way home and J. B. looked at me and said, "Preacher, I've been thinking about that sermon at prayer meeting and that was one of the best sermons I have ever heard."

I said, "J. B., no, you're wrong. I was wrong last night and you were right." So we got in a fuss over who was right last night! I'm just saying, we got back together. Why? Because we were winning souls together.

Jesus said in John 15, "Ye have not chosen me, but I have chosen you." Sometimes folks ask me about predestination. Yes, I believe I was chosen before the foundation of the world — *to get somebody saved.* That is what it says. It says, "I have chosen you, that ye should go and bring forth fruit, and that your fruit should remain: and that whatsoever ye shall ask of the Father in my name, he may give it you." Then

it says, "These things I command you, that ye love one another." What? Going and bringing forth fruit. Why? That
will make you love one another. So soul winning is the crux
of it all.

I tell my preacher boys in my church, "If you go to a
church where they are about to vote you out, kick you out,
go out and win enough folks to carry the vote right quick."
I was called to a church one time — in fact, the first full-time
church I ever had. I carried the vote about 25 to 17. When
I got there the first Sunday, a lot of my folks were gone.
Usually the first Sunday at the church you present yourself
for membership, but I didn't have enough folks there to
vote me in and I was already pastor. So I didn't join. I went
out winning souls and won eighteen or twenty the first few
weeks, then I joined the church. I had enough then to vote
me in. So it will take care of your problems.

This matter of soul winning is consuming to me. To me
it is just the biggest thing. It consumes me with the bigness,
and that anybody can do it. I wish I could tell you about
some experiences of folks who do it.

I know a fellow in Texas who, when he got converted,
couldn't even spell Jesus. The first year he won 169 to Jesus.
He picked up a hitchhiker and tried to witness to him. The
hitchhiker shook his head. He then talked real loud, but
the hitchhiker pointed to his ears and shook his head. So
this new convert started writing the Gospel out and the
hitchhiker pointed down and shook his head. He couldn't
read, he couldn't hear, he couldn't talk. So this soul winner,
who went to the third grade and couldn't even spell Jesus,
stopped the car and got out, took his Bible, pointed to the
Bible, pointed to his heart, pointed to Heaven, made a
motion to open your heart and let Him come in, got on his
knees and began to pray. The deaf and dumb fellow got
on his knees and mumbled a bit, got up with a smile of
Heaven on his face, pointed to the Bible, pointed to Heaven
and pointed to his heart.

I'm just saying, anybody can do it. This is a chance for you. As Dr. Bob Jones, Sr., says, God doesn't have many today. This is a chance for you. God is hard up and He will even use you.

1. Have a Definite Time to Go

This is one of the most important things in soul winning. If you are to be a soul winner, you have to do it on purpose. You must plan to do it. You must try to do it.

Let me encourage you a bit. I'm sure I speak for others; I know I speak for myself. There never is a day when I want to go soul winning. We're all made of the same clay and have the same weaknesses. Soul winning is a spiritual matter and the flesh will fight against it. In the summer it is too hot to go. Besides, folks are taking naps and it will make them mad if we wake them up. In a few months it is going to start snowing and we don't want to go out in the snow because we will catch cold talking through the door, and they would catch cold, too. There is never a good time to go.

Let me say this, though. I never want to quit once I start. In soul winning you have to have a self-starter. You have to start against the grain. You must start because you are supposed to start. I get tired of folks saying, "Dear Lord, give me a burden to win souls." While you wait on the burden, go out and win a few. The Lord didn't tell you to win souls if you have a burden; He said to win them anyway. If you don't want to, win them; if you feel like it, win them. If we went soul winning every time we felt like it, not a one of us would ever go, because Satan will try to keep us from it. He will keep you at your desk. You may become a great theologian studying things that are good to know, but the Devil will use them to substitute for soul winning.

So have a schedule. The trouble with most preachers — and I'm guilty of it myself — is that we don't live a disciplined life. Every preacher should have a schedule and try to live by it. Every preacher, every Christian should have a set time in the week or several times in the week when he does soul winning.

Personally, I try to go every Thursday afternoon, every Friday afternoon, and sometimes on Saturday. If I cannot go or do not go one of those times, I substitute another time. I suggest the layman should go when the church has visitation, if possible, and maybe one other time in the week. If you cannot go on visitation night, go another time, but set aside a time and say, "This is my time to win souls." If you do not, you will probably be a failure.

2.   Be Soul-Conscious

What does it mean to be soul-conscious? Talk to anyone any time or, better still, talk to everyone every time. Realize that everybody has a soul. The drugstore clerk, the barber, the shoeshine boy, the beautician, the grocery clerk, the milkman, bread man, service station attendant needs the Lord and we should witness to them.

Nobody is going to do it every time. It never gets easy to ask, "Are you a Christian?" I practice it. In front of the mirror I say, "Are you a Christian? Are y-o-u a Christian? Have you been converted? Are you saved?" I get in the habit of it. I don't care who you are; I don't care where you are, it is never easy.

For example, you go to buy medicine from the druggist. Well, you preachers are pretty nice-looking fellows — you could be mistaken for lawyers. You say, "Hello. How are you today?" The druggist thinks, "Isn't that a fine fellow." You know that if you ask, "Are you a Christian?" his opinion of you will change and he will think you are a nut, and nobody wants to be a nut. So you just don't say anything.

Now you had better get in the habit of asking, "Are you a Christian?" You will win more if you just start witnessing everywhere you go. You will win as many on the side as you do on purpose, and you will have the most wonderful experiences. If you preachers would start winning souls everywhere you go, you wouldn't have to get a book of illustrations to preach from next Sunday. Instead of saying, "In a distant city many years ago a certain man down a certain street..."you could say, "Last Friday morning out on the field I won somebody to Jesus. Let me tell you about it." It will liven up your sermons. That way you won't repeat anybody's illustrations. They will all be yours.

So, be soul-conscious. I mean by being soul-conscious, make it a habit of asking people everywhere you go, "Are you a Christian?" Ask the bread man, the school teacher, the milkman, the fellow who works in the yard, the telephone man, the fellow who reads the meter for the gas and electricity. Just ask everyone you see, "Are you a Chrstian? Have you been saved?" Be soul-conscious.

Let me give you this illustration. I was out mowing the yard one day while pastoring in Texas. Our church was the largest church in our city. One out of seven people in town belonged to our church. I saw my members quite often. Now, when I mow the yard, I'm not quite a beauty queen! That day I had on a tee shirt with a hole in the shoulder, and one right under the arm; I had on a pair of old tennis shoes with holes in them, and a pair of trousers with patches in the knee, and I think I had on either a golf cap or a fishing hat. I was a tragic-looking thing, a sight to behold!

My wife came out in the yard and said, "Honey, would you go get some sugar from the neighbor down the street?" I said, "All right, I'll do it." So I got the cup and marched down there with my tennis shoes on, and a hole in my breeches and tee shirt, and a fishing cap on. We were very close friends to the folks, so we never knocked. They would come in our house and we would go in theirs — just real close neighbors.

So I walked in and said, "Hey! Anybody home?" And there was — thirteen people at home — company all dressed up in suits and fine clothes. There I was. Imagine, Rev. Hyles, a cup in his hand, fishing hat on, split tee shirt, patch in his breeches, and a pair of tennis shoes on his feet! And I said, "Hello." The lady looked at me, she looked at her company, then announced, "This is my pastor." I was horrified! I was humiliated! I wanted to evaporate but couldn't.

Finally I said, "Excuse me; I'm sorry." Then I got to thinking. Shoot! Just take over the conversation. Just act like you have good sense. So in I walked. "How do you do! How are you? Are you a Christian?" I went around the entire room asking the same question. Then *they* got embarrassed.

(I found out long ago that when a preacher goes to a hospital or gets some place where he feels like a fifth wheel, he should just bluff them and take over the conversation. That will help you, too. It really will. You go to the hospital. Here is the doctor, the nurse, the family. And everybody says, "That's the preacher." You know how you feel, pastors. It's a terrible feeling. So I walk in, "Hello Doc. How are you?" Make *him* feel bad. Make *him* feel like he's a fifth wheel.)

So I walked in and asked each person if he or she were a Christian. The last man, a young man, said, "No, I'm not, but I've been thinking about it." Well, I said, "I can help you think about it right here." We knelt there in that home and opened the Bible. He got converted. He lived at Irving, Texas, forty miles from Garland. I said, "Now, J. D., you need to walk the aisle in the church in Irving tomorrow." He said, "If you don't mind, Preacher, I'll just stay over tonight and come to your church and walk the aisle." He did, and that night he got baptized in my church. Later he joined the First Baptist Church of Irving, Texas.

You don't realize how many places you will bump into people. I saw a lady while on vacation just recently. She said, "Hello, Brother Jack. Remember when you won me to the Lord?" I said, "I certainly do." It happened while I was looking for a Mrs. Marsh. I knocked on Mrs. Marsh's door — I thought. She came to the door. I said, "Mrs. Marsh?"

"No, I'm Mrs. Tillet."

I said, "Mrs. Tillet, I thought Mrs. Marsh lived here."

"No, she lives five houses down the street."

"Thank you, Mrs. Tillet." I walked off. Then I said, "Wait a minute, Mrs. Tillet. Are you are Christian?" She began to cry. I led her to Christ right there.

I have won shoeshine boys and fellows on airplanes. I was going to Phoenix to a conference last year. I sat down beside a man seventy-two years old, a wealthy rancher. "Where do you live?" I asked.

He said, "On a ranch between Phoenix and Tucson."

I said, "Do you and your wife live alone?"

"My wife died a few months ago."

I asked, "Do you ever think about having anybody else come and live with you?"

"Oh," he said, "If I could find somebody who would come and live with me, a friend to keep me company, I'd give anything in the world." He had chauffeurs, servants. He owned a big ranch with hundreds of acres, but was as lonely as he could be.

I said, "I know Somebody who would come and live with you."

"You do? Does He live in Phoenix?"

I said, "He sure does. He lives everywhere."

He said, "Who is it?"

"Jesus will come." In fifteen minutes that man had Somebody to go home with him to live.

Oh, if we will just take time to witness. The trouble is, we are ashamed of Jesus. We don't mind saying, "Isn't it hot today?" or, "I wonder how the Berlin situation is." We don't mind talking about Khrushchev. We're more eager to talk about him than about Jesus. Isn't that a shame! Here we are redeemed. He died for us on the cross. We have been made heirs of God and joint heirs with Jesus Christ. He is building a home in Heaven for us. We're God's children and we won't even tell a stranger that we belong to the Lord Jesus. Be soul-conscious.

3. Be Clean and Neat

There are two or three things a soul winner ought to watch. A soul winner ought to always watch his odor. That is tremendously important. Not only watch about your body odor, but you ought to be careful about your breath. One thing that will hurt more than most anything else in soul winning is bad breath. I would suggest that you carry mints with you. We men have a little pocket on the inside of our pocket. Put some mints in there. I always put one in my mouth before I conduct the invitation on Sunday and meet folks at the altar. So keep some mints handy.

There are other ways you can help your breath. Gum is good if you chew it when no one sees you. Someone said the only difference between a gum-chewing flapper and a cud-chewing cow is the intelligent look on the face of the cow! You can also use Sen-Sen. I used to get a bottle of Listerine to keep in my car and between each visit I gargled.

A soul winner should also be neat. Too often the world's conception of a soul winner is some fellow on a street corner, in a suit that doesn't fit; his tie is turned around; he has a funny look in his eye; his collar is turned up; and he is looking at you saying, "You'd better get borned agin or you're going to Hell." Don't you think God could use some folks who know how to dress neatly? Don't you think God could use somebody with a clean white shirt as well as a dirty shirt? Don't you think God could use somebody who knows how to comb his hair as well as somebody with messed-up hair? Don't you think God could use somebody who knows how to brush his teeth as well as somebody who doesn't?

Now I thank God for everybody who witnesses. I appreciate the sign on the back of a car. I admire every fellow who stands up and says, "You'd better get borned agin or you're going to Hell." I am grateful for every sign on a rock that says, "Jesus Saves." But I will say this: We need more people with some intelligence and a nice appearance, a nice personality, a good approach, to go into homes and tell people about Jesus Christ.

One should dress just as nice to go soul winning as he would to go to church. Men should at least wear a white shirt and a tie. I suggest you ladies wear high heels and hose. Dress as nicely as possible when you represent Jesus. When you go soul winning, you should give the best appearance. Someone has said, "I want to look so no one will ever accuse me of being a preacher, but they won't be surprised if they find out I am." So dress the part. Be clean and neat.

4. Carry a Testament With You

Personally I think it much better to carry a Testament than a Bible. Now do not be ashamed of the Bible, but if you plan to shoot a fellow, don't carry your gun out in the open up to his house. The best thing to do is to conceal your weapon. If I were going to shoot you, Dr. Rice, I wouldn't say, "Dr. Rice, here I come. Here's my gun. Here you are. Bang! Bang!" Dr. Rice would be out of the way by the time I got there. Now when some folks see you walking up the sidewalk with a big Bible, they will be hiding in the closet by the time you get there. If you have done much soul winning, you know what I'm talking about. Simply get out of the car and walk up to the door with a concealed Bible or Testament. Walk up the sidewalk with a big Bible and people will say, "Here comes the preacher." Mama says, "Tell him I'm not home." So the little fellow comes to the door and says, "Mama told me to tell you she wasn't home!" Now the reason is, they have you spotted.

But I get out of the car with a little Testament tucked away in my pocket, walk up to the door and since they don't know who it is, I have an inroad. When you go to win souls, the best thing is to keep your weapon concealed until you get into the house.

Carrying two Testaments is good also. I don't do this as religiously as I used to, but I did for years. You can buy inexpensive ones for about 25 cents. Let the lost person read from one and you read one. After you win him to Christ, give it to him as a souvenir. You can write on the inside that it was given to So and So on such and such a date (the date of the conversion), with a "Glod bless you" and a Scripture verse. Give him a Testament and keep one yourself. On occasion you might use his Bible if you see it around.

I don't sit beside the person when I win him. I used to. Now I sit across the room. Two or three reasons why. One, it is always best to sit across the room if you are dealing with the opposite sex. Then it is best to look in the person's eyes when taking to him.

5.   Go Two by Two

There are many reasons why we go two by two. It is scriptural. Jesus sent the apostles out two by two. One can encourage the other. There is something about strength in unity. If you don't believe it, eat at a restaurant by yourself tonight and try to witness to the waitress. Then tomorrow night go with Dr. Rice and me and see how much easier it is.

Another reason of primary importance. Jim Lyons and I were visiting in a home the other day (I'm the pastor and he is my assistant). The fellow took a liking to Jim. I don't know why but he wouldn't talk to me. He looked at Jim all the time. I moved around a little closer but still he looked at Jim. I said, "Yes, that's right"; still he wouldn't look at me. I wanted to say, "Hey, I'm the pastor; he's second in command." He still looked at Jim. That fellow wouldn't know me if he saw me on the street.

Now, Jim had to talk to him. What am I supposed to do?

The one who seemingly has the best inroad should carry the conversation and the partner should keep the road clear for the conversation. That is basically why two ought to go together.

I believe in being spiritual. It is wonderful to praise God, but you have to start where they are instead of where you are. I was out visiting one day with a wonderful Christian fellow. We knocked on the door. He said, "How do you do. My name is Jones (I'll call him that). Praise the Lord! This is Brother Hyles. Bless His holy name! We are here to tell you about Jesus. Glory to God! Are you saved? Hallelujah!" The man we went to see slammed the door in our faces. You must make them realize if they get what you have, it won't be so bad. So one makes the inroad while the other keeps the road clear.

What do we mean by keeping the road clear? We mean when the baby starts crying, you should change his diaper; when the beans start boiling, you put some water in them or turn the fire off; when the doorbell rings, you answer it; when the children start screaming for water, you get them a drink.

If you are not doing the talking, you be quiet until your partner is finished. The one doing the talking should do all the talking. Every now and then somebody says, "Well, that means when one runs out of something to say, the other can say something." Don't you go if you are going to run out of something to say. If you can't present the entire Gospel to a lost soul, you are not ready to go yet.

The fellow not doing the talking should keep the way clear. I have played every kind of game there is to play. I have done everything. I have changed many a diaper while out visiting. I have looked in every drawer in the bedroom hunting diapers so I could change a baby. That's right. I go to a house where there is a baby; the baby starts to cry while my partner is talking to the lost one. "Now, Mrs. Jones, never mind; I have four little children at my house. I have had babies at my house for ten years and I've changed hundreds of diapers. Let me take care of that." She says, "Oh! Brother Hyles...." "Now, Mrs. Jones, you sit right there and I'll take care of it." And I do. I have played soccer. I have played dolls. So many kids have been on my back at one time playing "piggy back" and "ride the horsie" that if my partner hadn't gotten the soul saved soon, I would have dropped over!

One day I went soul winning with Bob Keyes, who was then my assistant pastor, but who is now pastor of the church Dr. Rice founded in Dallas. Bob was an excellent soul winner and still is. We were out soul winning. I was doing the talking and the lady had a little baby who was acting ugly. About the time the lady was ready to get down to pray, the little boy said, "I want my bottle." Mama stuck the bottle in his mouth. "I don't want my bottle." She took it out. "I wanna bottle." She stuck it in. "I don't want my bottle." Then I prayed, "Lord, do something about this little rascal or he is going to mess up the whole thing." Do you know, he stopped and looked spellbound, as if he were in a trance. I said to myself, "Well, glory to God!" For about fifteen minutes that little baby didn't move. He didn't move his eyes; he just looked. The lady got converted and became one of the greatest Christians in our church.

When we left I said to Bob Keyes, "Bob, praise the Lord!"

He said, "Amen! Why?"

"Did you see what God did to that baby?"

He said, "What?"

I said, "All of a sudden, at the crucial time, that baby froze."

Bob said, "Well, I'm sure the Lord had something to do with it, but I may have helped a little because I had a ballpoint pen behind the coffee table going up and down, up and down, up and down. Preacher, I did that fifteen minutes and I'm worn out!"

Now, don't you think Bob had a part in that soul? Sure he did. Some of you spiritual giants need to know how to change diapers and handle ballpoint pens! You would get more people converted.

One time I was out with a fellow who got to praying for this lady, "Lord, save her! Lord, save her!" while I was trying to witness to her. He was talking louder than I was. Pretty soon he got on his knees and prayed, "Lord, save her!" Then he got on the floor and started beating the floor and saying, "Lord, save her!" I had to say, "Now, friend, I'm sorry but she can't hear what I'm trying to say. Would you mind going in the other room?" He did and we got her converted. If we are going to beat on the floor, let's do it at midnight, alone. If we are going to agonize, let's cry all night alone but not make a public demonstration or show. Do things that are necessary to do.

One night Bob Keyes was witnessing to a fellow and the doorbell rang. I said, "Dear friend, you stay right here. I'll answer the door." I went to the door. The fellow at the door said, "How do you do. Are you the man of the house?"

I said, "I'm a man of the house." (I was a man and I was of the house!)

He said, "I have an appointment with you to show you a vacuum cleaner." Obviously he had called and had an appointment.

I said, "I will be delighted to look at it. Come and we'll look at it on the front porch."

I didn't want the fellow to leave and I didn't want him to stay, so I saw all of the vacuum cleaner and its parts. We tested the thing out. Finally Bob Keyes said, "Hey, Jack! Come on. I've got him saved now."

I said, "Mr. vacuum cleaner man, my name is Hyles. I'm pastor of Miller Road Baptist Church and we just got this man converted. By the way, have you ever become a Christian?" We turned on him and tried to get him converted.

Now, if I hadn't kept that vacuum cleaner salesman occupied, this fellow would never have gotten converted. Keep your eyes open if you are the second party. Keep the way clear. Pave the roads in order for the person doing the witnessing to do the job. That's the reason basically for going two by two.

By the way, Dr. Rice told this morning how you can pray without ceasing. I imagine a fellow can pray and change the baby at the same time, don't you? We can pray and water the beans or play ball with the kids at the same time.

6. Go With Different People

Occasionally somebody will ask me, "Brother Hyles, if you started a new church or if you went to a new church, what is the first thing you would do in training the people to win souls?" The first thing would be to have different folks go with me to win a soul. The best way to train a soul winner is for him to watch someone else win a soul. The wonderful thing about soul winning is when you win a soul to Christ in the home, you are training a soul winner at the same time.

For example, let us suppose one brother gets converted in a church during preaching. That is wonderful. He is saved, but he has never seen a soul won in the home. Let's suppose another brother is won in his home. He has already seen me win him, so he knows exactly how to win someone else.

So, soul winning in the home reproduces itself. You train them and teach them how to become soul winners before they ever get converted. Now they can witness, and they can say, "At least I can do what Brother Hyles did to me." They already know basically what to do. So, go with different people so that others may watch you and learn.

7. Claim the Spirit's Fullness Before Going
Now I think basically that when a person goes to win

souls, he should spend his time winning souls. I had a secretary once who came to work about nine o'clock every morning, then she wanted to spend the first two hours praying. I think prayer is wonderful, but from nine to eleven in the morning is not the time for a secretary with a job to pray. From six to eight might be all right, or from 1 a.m. to 2 a.m., or from seven to nine at night. But she wanted to pray from nine to eleven in the morning. She thought I was unspiritual because I wanted her to type letters and get the work done. I said, "I don't mind you praying, but I'm not going to pay you for praying. Don't you pray on company time; you pray on your own time."

Now, soul-winning time should be time set aside for soul winning. We ought to set aside times for seasons of prayer, but not to borrow it from scheduled soul-winning time. When you go, say a simple prayer. I always pray basically this prayer, "Dear Lord, I claim in faith the fullness of the Holy Spirit before I go. I pray that You will help me to be a blessing to somebody and help me to win somebody today." Claim the Spirit's fullness — a simple prayer of faith asking God to help and give power. I make it brief.

Suppose you are going soul wining at one o'clock on Friday afternoon and you are going to pray for thirty minutes; pray from 12:30 to 1:00, not from 1:00 to 1:30. Do not steal soul-winning time. If you plan to go soul winning at one o'clock and you want to pray for four hours, start praying at nine o'clock in the morning and go soul winning at one. Stay on schedule about your soul winning and claim the Spirit's fullness before you go.

8. Go Believing

This one thing changed my soul-winning ministry. For example, people often take this little course, then call me on the phone to say, "Brother Hyles, it worked! It worked!" Sure it worked. Expect it to work. Isn't that what faith is?

Believe that God is going to save somebody. Expect to win them. Go believing. God said He would save sinners if you would go. That is His promise. "He that goeth forth and weepeth, bearing precious seed, shall doubtless come again with rejoicing, bringing his sheaves with him." Don't be surprised when God keeps His promise. Go believing.

9.   Be Nice

Be nice, courteous, kind and gentle. One thing so difficult for preachers is to change our behaviour from the pulpit to the living room. You can't act the same in the living room as you act in the pulpit. It is quite different, because you were not invited. You are infringing upon their privacy. When in the home be courteous and kind.

Many seem to think that the Lord said, "Go into all the world and teach all ladies to quit smoking cigarettes." Now I don't believe in smoking. We don't allow any deacons to smoke in our church. I don't believe in smoking, and especially in ladies smoking. However, God didn't send us out house to house to talk ladies into quitting smoking. God sent us out to get people converted. I've heard of preachers walking up to a door and addressing the lady thusly: "If you will throw that wicked weed away, I'll talk to you." This certainly is the wrong approach. Get her converted first; then perhaps she will throw her cigarettes away. In other words, don't get off the subject.

One day I was talking to a lady who said, "Brother Hyles, I can't be saved because I smoke. Do you think a person can be saved who smokes?"

I said, "That's a good question. Let's wait awhile and I'll discuss that with you." I said, "Do you realize that you are a sinner?"

"Oh, yes," she said, "but I'm not going to get saved because I'm not going to quit smoking."

I said, "All right, that's a fine question. We will wait awhile and I'll discuss that with you." So I told her how to be saved. I prayed and eventually she prayed and gave her heart to Jesus and was converted.

After she got converted I said, "By the way, you asked something awhile ago about smoking."

She said, "We took care of that when we prayed."

You will do a whole lot more good if you will keep on salvation, stay right on the line, and be nice and kind.

When you go to a home, be as courteous as a vacuum cleaner salesman or an insurance man. Be personable. I always say this: The first thing you have to do is win them to yourself. I don't mean you ought to selfishly try to make friends, then get them converted as a by-product. You have to first make them think you are all right. For example, you have to have a Christianity that they feel will fit them if they put it on. If you walk up saying, "Hello. Glory to God! How are you? Praise the Lord! Glad to see you. Hallelujah!" They say, "Oh, no! If I get what he's got, I'll probably be like he is; no thank you, I don't want it." A pleasant "How do you do. How are you?" is always in order. The first thought they should have is, "He is a nice fellow," or "She is a pleasant lady."

10. Be Complimentary

Everytime you go to a home, brag on something. We live in a selfish world. It is good to say, "You sure have a nice suit," or "Isn't that a precious child?" Make it a habit. Develop it inwardly. It should be part of your nature. One of the sins of the ministry is professional gratitude. Did you ever hear it? We often say, "Mrs. Jones, that was a good meal," but we don't mean a word of it. Stop and think. Mrs. Jones started cooking two days ago. She made her husband put his shoes outside the door when he came in and walk in barefoot to keep the floor nice. Those poor little ones couldn't even come in the house. They couldn't even use a towel. They had to use paper towels for two days to keep the towels clean for the preacher. The poor little things ate boloney for three days before you came to save so the lady could buy the nicest center-cut roast. She got the finest of everything, put out her best china, her best silver, her best crystal. She is as nervous as a cat. The preacher is coming! Now listen, stop and think about that; then look at her when you finish the meal and with a heart full of appreciation, say, "Mrs. Jones, I know what you've done for this meal, and I appreciate, personally, the work you've done to make this possible." Take the professionalism out of it and make it a part of yourself to want to be grateful and expressive of gratitude to people in the home.

The best thing to brag on is children. Be able to compliment little children. Man, listen, I can come in your home and say a few things about your young'uns and I'm a great fellow, regardless of what I've done wrong.

We had an insurance man in Texas who used to bother me to no end. He would say, "If you loved your family, you'd have more insurance." I would answer, "If I loved my family, I would sell what I've got now and spend the money to buy food for them." I hated to see him coming.

One day I was out in the yard and I saw him coming. I walked out to the curb and waited for him. When he stopped, I leaned against the door on his side, grinned at him and said, "Hello." He didn't even look at me. He looked at my little five-year-old girl and said, "Hello, sweetheart. You're the prettiest little girl I ever saw."

I said, "Isn't she though."

My little boy came toddling out (he was three at the time) and the salesman said, "Hello there, son. You're a fine-looking fellow. Have some chewing gum."

I said, "Won't you get out and come in?"

Sure, he knew how to get in. He bragged on the children. I think a man who has that good judgment about children deserves to come in! So he came in.

You do the same thing. Brag on the children. Compliment the home. If there is a new piece of furniture in the house, a beautiful carpet, a nice sofa or a dresser, brag on it. Be on the lookout for things to compliment.

11.   Be Careful About Going in

Now this I think is important. I do not try usually to go into the home unless the people are unsaved. If the people are saved, normally I do not go in. I don't chit-chat much with the saints. When I go out to visit I usually make twenty visits in one afternoon. That is four hours' work. The way I do that is to find out quickly if they are saved, pass the time of day very briefly, invite them to church and say good-by. Too many of us go out to visit and when we find a good Baptist fellow who tithes, makes a big salary, and one whom we want in our church, we go in and spend the afternoon, drink coffee, eat cake and let the world go to Hell. I do not personally spend a great deal of time visiting with saints. I just keep going and keep going until I find the lost ones and spend my time with them.

Also, if it isn't the opportune time, don't go in. I would especially be careful about going in if the opposite sex is alone. Now a word to you men who find a lady alone. Be very careful about going in. Sometimes if the person is busy, it is good to ask her if you could make an appointment to come back later at her convenience. But be careful about going in.

12.   Be a Good Listener

Talk about jobs wanted and positions open. There is lots of room in the world for some good listeners; there are many available positions open for good listeners. Did you ever hear a person say, "He sure is a fine fellow. Just a quiet, fine fellow. He is such a good listener"?

So often this happens — you preachers know this is true. A lady comes into my office. "Brother Hyles, I need some advice. I just don't know what to do. I felt like you could tell me what to do."

"All right; present your problem."

She talks and talks for an hour or so. I say nothing but, "God bless you. Uh huh. Well, yes."

That is all I say for an hour. She gets up and says after an hour, "Brother Hyles, you always have the best advice. You always know just what to do."

Well, I didn't advise anybody about anything. She just wanted somebody to unload on. That is one of the basic jobs of the pastor. Day after day they come through my office, as they do yours, wanting somebody to hear about their problems and burdens.

Go to a home and say, "Where do you work, Mr. Jones?"

"Down there at the steel company."

"What do you do down there?"

"Well, I make steel."

"How long have you been down there?"

"I've been there six months," Mr. Jones says.

"Where are you from?" I ask.

"I'm from Tennessee."

"Tennessee? That's a beautiful state. I've been down in the Cumberland Mountains in Tennessee."

Talk to him about his interests, and let him talk to you. Ask him about his family, where he is from. Ask him where he works. Let him talk to you for a while. Personally, I'm not an advocate of quick witnessing. Some of the best soul winners I know are, but I differ with them here. I think it best to chit-chat for awhile and be folksy. Listen to them. Let them present their problems, then after awhile talk to them.

Not long ago my wife and I were going to Colorado where I was preaching in a conference near Pueblo. We were on a jet going to Denver. The wife was sitting next to the window, I was sitting in the middle, and a businessman was sitting by me. I started a conversation with him. "What kind of business are you in?" He talked to me for thirty minutes. I have never heard so much talking in my life. I didn't have any idea what he was talking about. I just tried to act intelligent. There are a lot of basic answers, you know. He would say, "What do you think about the geophysical problem in the United States?"

I would answer, "It's really a problem, isn't it?"

He would say, "How do you feel we are economically?"

"Oh, I feel like we've seen better days, but we've seen worse days too, you know." Just a few basic questions and answers!

Finally after he unloaded for about thirty minutes, I got to talk to him. My wife punched me and grinned. She knew what I was doing. After we got off the plane she said, "You rascal! I knew the whole time you didn't understand a thing he was saying but you were waiting for the time when he would do the listening for awhile." If he talked to me for thirty minutes, then wouldn't let me talk to him for five minutes, he wouldn't have been very kind, would he? You listen to them for awhile and you will get them to listen to you easier. Be a good listener.

13. Only One Do the Talking

I wish I could stress this more. When two go together and both want to talk, it is often because of trying to argue people into becoming Christians. You can't do that. The best thing to do is to ask the dear Lord to help and lead and open doors, then with a kindly, gracious, Christian spirit, go into the homes and present the plan of God to the people, giving them a chance to accept or reject.

Only one do the talking. The one who has the inroad should do the talking. Suppose Dr. Rice, that you and I are going soul winning and we meet a fellow who is mowing his yard. I walk up and start talking to him. "Hey, neighbor! You've got your yard looking mighty nice."

He says, "Well, thank you."
I say, "What kind of mower is that?"
"Oh, it's a Jacobson," he replies.
"This is a good lawn mower," I say.
He says to himself, "This is a nice fellow."
Suppose we meet a man who is working on his car. "Hello, how are you?" I ask, putting forth my hand.
"Oh, my hand is greasy," he says.
"I don't care. I have shaken greasy hands before."
He thinks, "That sure is a nice fellow."

Be folksy and get his attention. Then the person who has the inroad can do the talking.

For example, Dr. Rice has written some books. If the fellow says he is an author, then I say, "Dr. Rice here has written scores of books." Immediately he becomes interested in Dr. Rice. Then I had better go water the beans; Dr. Rice is going to talk to him. So, I'm going to keep my mouth shut. The best thing for me to do is to be quiet, prayerful and helpful, then if he fails, I may try. Again I say, only one do the talking.

I went soul winning with a man one time, a wonderful Christian and a great fellow, but he didn't know a thing about soul winning. We went to a lady's house. She came to the door. I said, "How do you do. How are you today? Nice baby. Beautiful day. You have a nice home," etc. We talked awhile, then I asked, "Lady, have you ever become a Christian?"

"Well, I was baptized down in Henderson, Texas."

"Oh," he interrupted, "Henderson, Texas? I had a meeting down there. Do you know Zeb Peabody who runs the feed store there?"

I said, "Now lady, have you ever received the Lord and been converted?"

She said, "Well, one time I thought I did down in Jacksonville."

"Jacksonville?" he interrupted. I had four meetings in Jacksonville. Well, I'll declare! Jacksonville!"

Well, I had to send him home. He just couldn't be quiet. You just let one person do the talking. The one who gets the inroad should follow right on through and present the plan while the other one keeps the way clear.

14. Stay on the Subject

Now, the place the Devil will ruin more soul winners than most any other place is here. I sometimes think that knowing too much hurts soul winners. If we could just keep it simple and stay on the simple plan of salvation, we would do a lot better. I spent many days in school learning to handle a Mormon; I haven't seen but two since I got out of college. I memorized Scripture after Scripture on how to handle special cases. A Mormon will often handle just like a Jehovah's Witness. A Catholic will often handle just like a Seventh-Day Adventist. To learn how to win an unbeliever is the big thing. And the simple plan of salvation is the answer. Just stay on the subject.

Suppose the old question is asked — "Where did Cain get his wife?" What should I do? I would say, "That's a good question, and I will tell you what we will do. I'll make a note of it and we will discuss it when we get through. Now, down here in Romans 3:10. . . ."

Just stay right on the subject. You say, "Brother Hyles, what if he asks you a question about Heaven or Hell?" You are going to tell them about Heaven and Hell in a minute anyway. Tell them the same thing: "That's a good question." You plan the speech, and don't let anything he says get you off the main line. Don't spend your time answering his questions or he will be governing the conversation. You govern the conversation. You carry the ball. Stay on the subject.

15. Find Someway to Get Them Lost

Let me explain. Often I've gone out to win souls and asked, "Are you a Christian?" If he said, "Yes, I am," I would let it go at that. But some people will answer yes to "Are you a Christian?" who are not really Christians and you need to get the Gospel to them. To do this, we must get to a verse like Romans 3:10. I've got to figure some way to get to Romans 3:10 and get them to let me tell them how to be saved. Do you see what I mean?

Let me illustrate. A family comes to talk to me and I know they are lost. "Brother Hyles, we have a home problem. Do you know any Bible verses that would help our home?"

"Ah, yes. There is a verse in the Bible that will help anybody's home. Turn to Romans 3:10."

Somebody comes in, "Brother Hyles, my business is going bankrupt. What does the Bible say about business?"

"Ah, it says a great deal about business. The best Scriptures about business in the Bible begin at Romans 3:10." Then tell them about Jesus. He will solve any problem.

Now, let me give you an illustration that will prove what I am trying to say. This is the only time that it has ever happened but it is a most vivid illustration to explain this point.

I went to visit a family. Let's call the name Hill. It was up on the second floor of an apartment building. They had three lovely children. I walked in and said, "How do you do, Mr. Hill. Are you a Christian?"

"Oh, yes," he said. "I was saved when I was three years old."

Well, I didn't know what to say. Then I asked Mrs. Hill, "Are you a Christian?"

"Oh yes," she said. I was saved when I was a baby."

Well, now I didn't think they were saved. If they had said they weren't Christians, I could have showed them

Romans 3:10 but I couldn't when they said they were Christians. So I asked, "Have you been born again?"

Oh, yes; both of them were born again. He was born again when he was three; she was born again when she was a baby.

"Have you been converted, saved?"

That's right; they had been saved.

"If you died, do you know if you would go to Heaven?"

Yes, yes; they knew if they died they would go to Heaven.

Well, I didn't know what to do. I wanted to get to Romans 3:10. So I said, "Well, let me ask you this: Do you ever wish you knew how to pray? If I could show you some Scriptures on prayer, would you be willing to learn how to pray better?"

I was going to show them a good Scripture about prayer — Romans 3:10 — but she said, "Oh, we have family altar and private devotions; we took a correspondence course on prayer recently."

"Well," I said, "did you ever wish you had a Bible study, some Scriptures to show you how to study the Bible?"

If they had said, "No, we don't study the Bible much," I was going to say, "Listen, there are some Scriptures that will unlock the entire Bible and the first one is Romans 3:10."

But she said, "Oh, yes; we are taking a Bible course right now, a correspondence course."

I tried every way I could to get to Romans 3:10, but I couldn't do it. I said, "Well, is your home what it ought to be? Would you love to have some Scriptures on the home — how to have a better home and a good Christian home?" I was going to show them Romans 3:10 — how it would lead you to have a better home, etc. I couldn't do it, so I prayed, "Lord, help me." Finally I said, "This is a good home. You have been born again; you are converted; you have been saved; you pray and you are taking Bible study courses. You know, there is one thing that a home like this ought to have."

They asked what.

I said, "A formal dedication service."

Now that sounded good to them, and Mr. Hill said, "Honey, that sounds real good. When could we schedule that?"

I said, "It so happens that I have one of the services with me right now."

He said, "Could we do it here?"

I said, "We can do it right here."

Listen, she went in and changed clothes, combed her hair, put clean little dresses and shirts on the children. They came in like a group going to Sunday School. I said, "Now, then, we're going to read some Scriptures on home dedication. It says in Romans 3:10, "As it is written, There is 'no home' righteous, no, not one." In Romans 5:12 it says that sin came into the first home and it was the first home that brought the first curse upon man. I went through the same old Scriptures, Romans 3:10, 5:12, 6:23, 5:8, and I said, "Those are Scriptures about the dedication of the home.

Now would you like to pray a prayer of home dedication?"

They said that would be real nice. So we all got on our knees. I prayed and then said, "Mr. Hill, you want to pray a prayer of dedication for your home, don't you?"

"Yes, sir," he said.

I said, "Mr. Hill, this is the prayer to pray: 'Dear Lord, be merciful to me a sinner and forgive my sins and save my soul. I do now repent of my sins and trust Jesus to save me.' "

He prayed the prayer. She prayed the same prayer.

We got off our knees and they were both crying. I said, "That's wonderful! Now you said you were saved when you were three, didn't you?"

Mr. Hill looked at me and said, "No, I just got saved a minute ago."

That is a long way around to get the Gospel to them without them wanting it if you don't think they are saved.

Let me say this also. If you can't get it to them, I have what

I call a long plan and a short plan. In the long plan I read the Scriptures; in the short plan I quote them. For example, I say, "Would you like to be a Christian?"

He says, "No, I don't think I would."

I say, "If I were to show you in the Bible, would you be willing to look at it?"

"No," he says.

"Well, let me ask you *this* question." (Now that is the secret. Every soul winner ought to learn that little sentence, "Let me ask you *this* question.") I was previously going to take the Bible and show him these Scriptures, but he says he doesn't want to see them. So I say, "If you don't want to know the plan, let me ask you *this* question: Do you realize that Romans 3:10 says that there is none righteous, no, not one"? I'm doing the same thing that I was going to do. He thinks, "Boy, I sure got him off the subject; he is not going to show me how to get saved." He thinks you are off the subject.

So if you can't use the long method, use the short method. Just back up and take another path and go at him from another direction, but get the plan to him. Then you can go to him with the short method where you quote the same Scriptures but do not read them.

16. Stay in the Same Book of the Bible

This is important. Use the same book all the way through. Some books in the Bible you could use for the plan of salvation are: Romans, John, First John, Isaiah, Psalms, Acts, Ephesians, etc. Definitely it is best to stay in the same book in the Bible and not jump around too much.

Here is the way I do it and I think this is a good suggestion. When I start talking to a person I say, "Now, Mr. Jones, the Bible is composed of 66 books and each book has a different immediate purpose. For example, the book of Genesis explains the creation of man. The book of Revelation explains the end time. There is one book in the Bible that is given especially to tell about the power of the Gospel of Christ and how to go to Heaven. That is the book of Romans. This book clearly explains how to go to Heaven."

What you are doing is this: You are saying to him, "Now, I'm taking you to that part of the book that specializes in telling you how to go to Heaven." It makes him feel you are an expert.

One thing I always try to do in a town where I pastor; I always try to make folks think of me as a specialist. All pastors should be specialists on soul winning, but I try to make folks think of me as a specialist. Folks call me all the time and say, "Brother Hyles, would you go to the hospital and see my lost loved one or send your assistant pastor to see him?"

"Well, yes," I say. "Do you belong to a church in town?"
They answer, "Yes, I belong to a certain church."
"Oh, is your pastor out of the city?"
"No, but he doesn't specialize in getting folks saved," they say.

I don't say a word about it. I just want to create the attitude in town that my church is primarily a place to get folks converted. It is important to build that kind of atmosphere. You would be surprised how many people who maybe wouldn't like you personally and wouldn't want to join your church, but they know you try to get folks converted.

For example, here is a lady who has an unsaved husband. He is a drunkard and won't go to church with her. One night he says to her, "Honey, I think I'll go to church with you tonight."

So she says, "Well, wonderful."
He says, "Let's go to your church."
She says, "Let's don't go to my church tonight; let's go somewhere new. Let's go to First Baptist and hear Brother Hyles. Would you like to do that?"

She knows we will try to get him saved. They might be having a special activity at her church, but she knows at our church we will try to get him converted. I'm saying that if you will build that reputation, you will get a lot of folks converted who may not stay in your church, but you will develop the reputation as the evangelistic headquarters in town.

So, I would suggest you try to lead the folks to know that you know what you are talking about and that you have found the book. Only use the one book.

17. Draw a Map in Your Testament

I contend that you can be a soul winner if you don't know a single verse of Scripture, if you can draw a map in your Bible to tell yourself where to go. All you need do is find Romans 3:10 and you won't have to know a single verse of Scripture. Right beside Romans 3:10, write the next verse to tell you where to go in your Bible. Actually what you do is draw yourself a little road map in your Bible to explain where to go next.

First, turn to Romans 3:10. That is all you have to remember. Underline the verse. Beside it write 3:23. After you have read Romans 3:10, it tells you where to go next. Now turn to Romans 3:23. Underline that verse and beside that write 5:12. Turn to 5:12 and underline 5:12 and write beside it 6:23. Underline 6:23 and beside it write 5:8. Underline 5:8 and write beside it 10:9-13.

Now that is a map for you. You don't have to know a single verse of Scripture to be a soul winner if you draw a map in your Bible. You follow the map until you learn the Scriptures. Of course, as you go along, you will learn many other Scriptures that will help, but these are basic ones.

18. Ask Them, "If You Died Now, Do You Know That You Would Go to Heaven?"

I think that is the best question that I have ever used.

Some use, "Do you know Jesus? Are you born again? Are you saved? Are you a child of God?" I try to avoid terminology that will be too religious for them. Many don't know that kind of terminology.

Basically there are only two religions in the world. One is the belief that salvation is all of God, and Jesus did it all on the cross; the other is that we have to do something to get converted. In this second you have combined all of the false religions. That is the old mystery of Babylon, mother of harlots in Revelation 17. Many religions are wrapped up in this one thing — that you have to do something to go to Heaven. Anybody who says you have to do something to go to Heaven, doesn't know if he is going or not. He usually says he thinks so or has a good chance or may go to purgatory. The only person who will tell you he knows that if he dies he will go to Heaven is the fellow who has trusted Jesus completely to save him. That is why I ask, "Do you know if you died you would go to Heaven? Do you know it?" Some ask, "Are you a Christian?" Almost anybody will say yes to this. I think that the best question is, "Do you know that if you died you would go to Heaven?" Now ask,

19. "Would You Like to Know?"
Now ask,

20. "If I Showed You How You Could Know, Would You Do What the Bible Says?"
It may be done thusly. "Now, Mr. Doe, let me ask you a question: Do you know that if you died this minute you would go to Heaven?"

"No, I don't believe I do."

"Let me ask you this: Would you like to know? Don't you think it would be fine if you could know that if you died you would go to Heaven?"

"Yes."

"Well, let me ask you this: If I could take this Bible and explain to you how you could know beyond any shadow of a doubt, that you could know right now, and you could see it and you could understand it, would you believe it? Would you do what the Bible says?"

Do you see what I'm trying to say? It is good to get him committed that he will do it; then you have gone a long way toward getting him saved before you ever present the plan. So these three questions: (1) "Do you know that if you died today you would go to Heaven?" (2) "Would you like to know?" and (3) "If I could show you how you could know, would you do it?"

21. Show Him That He Is a Sinner
For this, use Romans 3:10 and 3:23.

22. Show Him the Price on Sin
Show him this in Romans 5:12 and 6:23.

23. Show Him That Jesus Paid the Price
Use Romans 5:8.

24. Review the Main Points to Be Sure He Understands
I always use the following: "Now, Mr. Doe, there are only four things you must know to be saved. First, you must know that you are a sinner. For example, Romans 3:10 says, 'As it is written, There is none righteous, no, not one.' Let me illustrate. If there is none righteous, that means I'm not righteous, doesn't it? (Notice, I didn't get him unrighteous first; I got me unrighteous. Never put the sinner below you. You always let him know that but for the grace of God you would be in the fix he is in. You get yourself lost first.) So if there is none righteous, I'm not righteous. If there is none righteous, then Mr. Doe, you are not righteous. Also, it says, 'For all have sinned, and come short of the glory of God.'

Now if all have sinned, that means I've sinned — right? That means your wife has sinned, and that means you have sinned."

If he still acts like he is not a sinner, you just list a few sins and you will catch him. A lot of times I say this: "Now do you realize that you are a sinner? For example, the Bible mentions some sins such as evil thinking, bad literature, ugly disposition, etc." Somewhere along that line there will be something that he does. Show him that he is a sinner.

Second, show him the price on sin. Romans 5:12: "Wherefore, as by one man sin entered into the world, and death by sin. . . ." What kind of death? All death, both spiritual and physical death, the sum total of death. ". . . and so death passed upon all men, for that all have sinned." And Romans 6:23, "For the wages of sin is death. . . ." So there is a price on sin. What is that price? Death. What kind of death? That includes the second death of Revelation 20:14, and that second death is the Lake of Fire. So ultimately a person who is a sinner must pay for it by going to Hell. That is the basic price on sin.

Third, the next thing we must do is show that Jesus paid the price. So I say this: "Mr. Doe, God looked down from Heaven and saw that you were a sinner. He saw that you were in debt. He saw that you and I deserved to go to Hell. He wanted to save us and made a plan to do it. He came to the world Himself. His name was Jesus. He was God in a human body. For thirty-three years He lived here in this world. He did not commit one single sin. This is important. Mr. Doe, suppose that Jesus Christ had sinned one time only. The price on sin being death or Hell, where would Jesus have had to go when He died? The answer is Hell, but He did not sin. He did not commit one sin, but He went to the cross, and on the cross He suffered spiritual death when He said, 'My God, my God, why hast thou forsaken me?' He suffered the same thing that a lost person will have to suffer in Hell. I'll go farther than that. I believe that He suffered as much in that moment on Calvary as the sum total eternal suffering of all the lost people who will ever go to Hell to stay forever. Actually He was paying our price for our sins. He was becoming our substitute."

Fourth, "If we will receive that price as our hope for Heaven and receive Him as our Saviour from sin, He will make us His children and take us to Heaven when we die."

That's the review. You explain it to them first, then you review. Let me review it with you now. "Let me ask you a question, Mr. Doe. Do you realize that you are a sinner?"

"Yes, sir."

"Do you realize that people who die in their sins must go to Hell?" (Now be as severe with that as you can. If a sinner knows he is going to Hell, say, "Do you realize that if you died right now, you would go to Hell?" If he is a little sensitive about it, then you can say, "Do you realize that a man who dies in his sins goes to Hell?" Be as severe as you can but don't make your patient so sick you will kill him before you heal him. You have to stay with him.) "Do you realize that Jesus Christ has suffered your Hell already for you? If we knelt here together and had prayer and you sincerely received Christ as your Saviour, do you believe God would make you His child?"

That is the review. I have explained to him how to get saved, then I have reviewed and asked these questions.

25. Ask if You May Pray

There are several ways to do this, but you must try to get them to pray. If he is really ready, say, "Could I pray for you, and while I pray, would you pray and ask God to save you today?" Maybe he is not quite that ready. Maybe you don't know. You could say, "Could I pray that you will get saved?" Maybe you don't think he will let you pray for him to get saved. Then you say, "Could I have a word of prayer with you before I go?" Anyway, to get your head bowed is good. If you are talking to him, he might interrupt, but if you are talking to the Lord, he won't. You can preach him a little sermon in the prayer. If you can't win a fellow to Christ, and if he won't let you present the plan to him, the best way to tell him how to be saved is to tell the Lord and let the sinner hear you.

I go into a home and say, "Sir, would you like to know how to be saved?"

"No. Don't have time for it. The wife's sick and I'm busy."

"Could I have a prayer for your wife before we go, that she will get well?"

With his wife lying there sick, a man would be a fool not to let the preacher pray for her. He says, "Well, O.K."

I pray, "Dear Lord, bless this wife and make her well, and help this man to know that Romans 3:10 says, 'As it is written, There is none righteous, no, not one.' And if people die in their sins, according to Romans 6:23 'the wages of sin is death.' O dear Lord, show him that Romans 5:8 is true when it says that 'God commendeth his love toward us, in that, while we were yet sinners. . . .' "

Pray him the plan. He won't interrupt you. You can get by with a lot of things talking to the Lord that you wouldn't talking to him.

After you review, get to pray some way or another. If he will consider getting saved, good. If you can't get by with that, just get him to let you pray.

26. Ask Him to Pray

I stop abruptly in my prayer. I pray a simple prayer. Never pray a big prayer. You must pray a prayer so simple that he won't mind his prayer following yours. If you pray, "Jesus, Thou God of Jacob; oh, Thou God of Rehoboam and Jeroboam and Jehoshaphat; oh, Thou great God of the universe, the omnipotent, omnipresent, omniscient God, would you save this man?" After that, he won't pray. But you can pray this, "Dear Lord, here is a fellow who needs to get converted. I pray You will help him get saved. May he receive Christ. You love him, dear Lord. . . ." "Now fellow, will you pray?" You pray like that, and he can pray his little prayer in a minute.

I always stop in the middle of my prayer. I say, "Dear Lord, lead this man to be saved. You led me here and I pray that he will be saved today. May his wife have a Christian husband and the little children a Christian daddy. Make this be the day of his salvation. Now while our heads are bowed in prayer, Mr. Doe, would you be willing today to ask God to forgive you and tell Him you want to get saved?"

See, you stop in the middle of your prayer and lead him to pray. Let me say this: Fifty per cent of the time when you get this far the lost person is going to pray. Now, I would suggest you tell him what to pray but not the words. Like this: "Would you ask God to forgive you and tell Him you want to receive Jesus today?" Fifty per cent of the time he will make up a prayer. I've heard some of the sweetest prayers. A lot of times he won't pray. He does not know how to pray. He says, "I have never prayed before." In that case I say, "Mr. Doe, would you just say these words and mean them in your heart, 'Lord, be merciful to me a sinner . . . forgive my sins and save my soul . . . I now receive Jesus as my Saviour'?"

Let me say this: By the time you get there, the forces of Hell will be fighting you. By the time you get this far talking to a sinner, you will feel like everything you own depends on what you do right now. Realize the seriousness of it all.

27. Ask Him to Take Your Hand

He has just prayed and asked the Lord to save him. "Now Mr. Doe, while our heads are bowed, if Jesus Christ came in the room, He would extend His hand, no doubt, and ask you to take His hand if you would receive Him. Mr. Doe, if you will make this day the day of your salvation and this moment receive Christ as your Saviour, just like my hand were His hand, would you put your hand in mine?" Now, he takes your hand.

28. You Pray Again

"Our Father, help this man to see in his heart that salvation is by faith in the Lord Jesus Christ and what He did on Calvary. Give him peace in his heart and the assurance of salvation. In Jesus' name. Amen.

Before you pray that last prayer, you may do several things. For example, if the wife is in the room, have her come over and take his hand, too. Then ask little Johnny to come and place his hand on Mommy's and Daddy's. Then you can have your closing prayer.

29. Ask Him, "Where, According to the Bible, Would You Go if You Died Now?"

This is important. Many people, after they win a soul to Christ, ask; "How do you feel?" It doesn't matter how he feels. How he feels has nothing in the world to do with it. The average soul winner says, "Feel any better?" That doesn't make any difference. You will stand there and argue with a fellow and he will say, "I believe you have to feel it to get saved."

You say, "No, you don't. You don't have to feel it — it is by faith." Then the first thing you ask him after you pray is, "How do you feel?" Salvation doesn't depend on how you feel; it depends on if you are believing the Book. The minute you do what God says in His Book, you believe God will do what He says He will do in His Book, you are converted. It is by faith in what God says.

The question is, "According to the Bible, where would you go if you died now?"

The answer, "I'd go to Heaven."

The sweetest thing happened in our altar recently. A little lady came down to the front. She said she wanted to be saved. I prayed with her myself. Normally I don't do it, but I prayed with her myself. I asked, "Now where would you go if you died?"

She said, "Well, the Bible says I would go to Heaven."

"Where do you think you would go?"

"I think I would go to Hell," she said.

I said, "But the Bible says you would go to Heaven."

"That's right; it does say that," she said.

"Let me ask you a question," I said. "Did you ever tell a lie?"

"Oh, yes, I have told a lie."

"Does God ever lie?"

"No."

"All right, you say you are going to Hell, but God says you are going to Heaven. Whose word do you think I ought to take?"

She said, "I guess you'd better take God's."

"Now where do you think you would go?"

"I think I'd go to Heaven."

It is because God said it. Ask them, "According to the Bible, where would you go if you died now?"

30.   Lead Him to a Public Profession

31.   Go By and Get Him on Sunday Morning

32.   Sit With Him in the Service

But you say, "I sing in the choir." Well, you had better quit the choir that Sunday or let him sing with you. Sit with him in the service.

33.   Go Down the Aisle With Him

34. Within a Week Have Him Over for a Meal or Coffee and Cake or Something

He just got converted. "According to the Bible, where would you go if you died?"

"Heaven."

Use that as an excuse to call somebody. Call a loved one; call a friend. Tell your wife about it.

Randall F. was a pretty mean rascal, a drunkard, mean to his wife and everything. Kenneth, his brother, was a good Christian. We went to see Randall about one o'clock in the morning. Kenneth got so burdened about him. Randall got saved. He really got saved. And he has been a good Christian. He got his wife out of bed and rejoiced in the Lord and they praised the Lord together. We just lived it up.

Some of us preachers — a fellow comes down the aisle on Sunday and what do we do? We say, "Do you want to be saved?" "Yeh." The people never know what happened. It seems to me that if a person gets born again in your church, you ought to let folks know about it. Live it up. I had them come down Sunday and kiss each other. A man gets converted and his wife is already saved. "Come on down here with him. Bless the Lord. Give a word of testimony."

"Oh, thank God! My husband got saved today!" Kiss him. The Bible says to greet one another with a holy kiss, so she kisses him. All the young'uns come down and stand with Daddy. Daddy kisses his little young'uns. Bless God, they have got a Christian daddy now. Some preachers make it sound like it was the Statue of Liberty being dedicated. Live it up. Somebody got out of Hell! They're going to Heaven! Somebody got regenerated. Angels are singing. Folks are redeemed and going to Heaven, and not going to burn forever.

You in your ministerial cloak and croak, you get up there and the poor people don't even get one tear or one laugh before they go home. Isn't that a shame! I can't understand this dignified pomp and put-on when people are getting converted. We have more to shout about than anyone.

Here is a fellow — he is going to Heaven. Jesus has taken him ... salvation by grace ... can't fall ... can't lose it ... preserved, and we say, "Amen."

And here is a fellow — he is hanging on ... holding out ... hoping he won't slip and fall and slide, and he shouts all the way to Heaven. Isn't that something! It doesn't add up, does it?

Every once in a while folks will say that I preach like a Pentecostal. I wished they would say I preach like a Baptist. When I was a kid they did that. Nowadays they say "like a Pentecostal," because we have changed a great deal.

"All right, you have been saved now; you know you are converted; that if you died tonight you would go to Heaven. The next thing God wants you to do is to let people know that you have been saved. Read Romans 10:11, 'For the scripture saith, Whosoever believeth on him shall not be ashamed.' You believe on Him, don't you? You are not ashamed of Him, are you? The next thing God wants you to do is to make public your decision."

I always say something like this: "Mr. Doe, we could get a loudspeaker, drive down Main Street on Saturday afternoon and announce it to everybody, or we could have it printed up on circulars. But the usual way, Mr. Doe, is to come to church and when the preacher finishes preaching, come down the aisle to the front, have a seat on the front and let the preacher tell the people that you have been saved. Now, would you do that at some Bible-believing church this Sunday morning? If you would promise God, not me, but God, would you take my hand? Wonderful. Now, Mr. Doe, it just so happens that the wife and I come very close to here Sunday and we would love to have you as our guest Sunday morning. I'll be happy to come down the aisle with you to make it easy for you, and you can go with us and we can introduce you to some people, show you around. How about, say 9:15 Sunday morning? Wonderful."

I get them and take them with me to church. Before the Sunday School starts, I take them into the auditorium (especially if I think they don't know) and I stand back and say, "Now, Mr. Doe, this is the auditorium and there is the pulpit where I preach. I'm going to ask you to sit in the service about right over here. When I finish preaching, we're going to stand and sing a song. When we stand and sing that song, you will leave your seat, come down this aisle to the front and over to the center and I will take your hand. I will ask you to have a seat on the front. I will explain to the people what happened in your home this past week."

I tell him everything he is going to do. I do that in every invitation at my church.

On vacation recently I was in a church where I heard a marvelous message. When the pastor finished preaching, he said, "All right, we are going to stand and anybody who wants to be saved, come." We all stood but we didn't know where to come — whether to come to town, to the front, or to a party. If a fellow hadn't known what to do, he wouldn't have known where to come.

I say, "Now, if you want to be saved this morning, leave your seat, come to the nearest aisle, down the aisle to the front, give me your hand if you will give Christ your heart." Break it down in little pieces for them. So, before the service I tell them exactly how to make their public profession of faith.

Notice that up to this point I haven't mentioned joining the church. I often say nothing about joining the church until they are down the aisle. They will appreciate that, too. You will get the reputation of not being primarily interested in getting church members, but in getting people saved. Too many spend time telling you that the nursery is air-conditioned; they have a new educational building; and the young people have a good program, etc. I often do not talk to them about joining the church until after they make their profession. As soon as they make it public, my assistant pastor goes by and talks to everybody in the line. (By the way, we have them stand up in front and we shake their hands after we dismiss the service.) My assistant pastor talks to each one about getting baptized. My secretary has a letter in her hands and comes behind him. The letter explains what to bring at night and invites them to come to the baptism class at 6:30 on Sunday.

Now very briefly I am going to win Mr. Doe to Christ. He is at home and I am going to knock on the door. He is reading the newspaper and has his house shoes on. I knock on the door. "How do you do, sir. Mr. Doe, my name is Jack Hyles. How are you today? I'm glad to see you. Say, that's a cute child you have there. She's a doll. Would you like to have some candy, honey? Give me some sugar . . . Well, Mr. Doe, I hope you aren't too busy. I'd like to talk to you just a minute. I can come back later if it isn't convenient."

"No, I'm not busy; come in."
"Thank you."
"Have a seat," Mr. Doe says.
"Thank you."

We chit-chat a while and I ask him where he works and talk about his home town. (Let me say this: this is where a general education comes in. Every soul winner ought to know as much about every subject as he can and about every state and every job, etc. General knowledge will come in handy as you can talk intelligently about most any subject.) We talk about the weather, his job, etc.

I listen to him for a while, then I say, "Let me ask you this, Mr. Doe: Do you know that if you died today, you would go to Heaven?"
"No, sir."

"Let me tell you, it is a wonderful thing to know. Did you ever think you would like to know that if you died you would go to Heaven?"

"Yes, sir."

"Let me ask you this question: Do you feel that if I could show you in the Bible exactly how you could know that if you died you would go to Heaven, and if you could see it and understand it, would you be willing to do it?"

"Yes, sir."

"I'm glad you said that. I'm going to show you what the Bible says about becoming a Christian. Now, Mr. Doe, there are only four things basically that you have to know to be saved. The first thing is, you must know that you are a sinner. I want you to look there at chapter 3 and verse 10 if you would please, where it says. . . ."

(By the way, I hardly ever *quote* a lot of Scriptures myself. Act like you're reading it yourself. Don't ask him to read the Scripture if you think he might have trouble or that it might embarrass him. You are not there to show off; you are there to help him. A lot of times they might think, "Man, doesn't he know the Bible!" But that isn't what you are there for.)

"So, notice in verse 10, 'As it is written, There is none righteous, no, not one.' If there are none righteous, Mr. Doe, that means I'm not righteous, doesn't it? That means that you're not righteous, doesn't it?"

"Yes."

"Notice in verse 23, 'For all have sinned, and come short of the glory of God.' If all have sinned, that means I have sinned and that you have sinned. Is that right?"

"Yes, sir."

"Now, that is the first thing you must know — that you are a sinner.

"The second thing that you must know to be saved is that there is a price on sin. Look here if you will please, to

Romans 5:12 where it says, 'Wherefore, as by one man sin entered into the world, and death by sin; and so death passed upon all men, for that all have sinned.' Here is the story. God made a man, and his name was Adam. He made a woman, and her name was Eve. He put them in the Garden of Eden. He said that they could eat of every tree in the garden except one, and that was the tree of the knowledge of good and evil. He said that if they ate of that tree, they were going to die. They ate of that tree. Now every man is born in sin, is a sinner, and the Bible says that the price on sin is death. Look at verse 23 of chapter 6, and it explains the same thing, 'For the wages of sin is death. . . .' Here's what it means. When man sinned, he died spiritually. Now, if he is dead spiritually and he dies physically while he is dead spiritually, he will have to suffer the second death, and that is called the lake of fire."

(Now usually on this matter of Hell, I say, "Of course you believe in Hell. Some folks don't believe in Hell." If you say, "Of course you believe in Hell" he will hate to say he doesn't.)

"So that means a person who is a sinner must pay for it by suffering Hell. Do you understand that? That's the price on sin.

"The third thing that you have to know is that Jesus paid that price. Look at chapter 5, verse 8, if you will please, 'But God commendeth his love toward us, in that, while we were yet sinners, Christ died for us.' Now, what is the price on sin? Death. What did Jesus do for us? He died for us. That means He was paying our price for us. He was suffering our Hell. He came to earth from Heaven and became a man, never sinned one time. He did not owe the debt. He paid a debt that He didn't owe. You owe a debt that you have not paid. He has a plus one; you have a minus one. He says that He would like to take His plus one and put it against your minus one, and balance the equation.

"Now the question is, How can you get His plus over here on your side? That's the fourth thing. The first thing you must know is that you are a sinner. The second thing, that sinners go to Hell when they die. The third thing, that Jesus has paid the price for sinners. The fourth thing, if you would be willing by faith to receive this plan as your hope for Heaven and Christ as your Saviour, He will take your sins and place them on His account and take His payment and place it against your sins and you would not owe for your sins anymore. Jesus paid the price for you.

"Let me illustrate. (This is one of the sweetest things usually that we do when we win souls. This is one of the most effective plans I have ever used.) Let's just say now that this is your record in Heaven, and your record is written in Heaven. Every sin you have ever committed is written in Heaven. Let's just list a few of your sins. Did you ever take anything that wasn't yours? Did you ever say a bad word? All right, let's list — bad word. Did you ever have an evil thought? All right, let's write it down — evil thought. We'll list some more.

"Now, what is the price on these things? The price tag is H-e-l-l, Hell. You're a sinner; here are your sins. That is Romans 3:10 and 3:23. Here is the price — Romans 5:12 and 6:23. Jesus went to the bank of Heaven and paid your debt for you. He sent me today to tell you about it. He has paid this price for you.

"Now, you have one of two choices. You can say, 'Preacher, I know He did but I don't want to do anything about it,' and you will still be in debt. Or you could say, 'Jesus, I know You died for me, You paid my Hell and I'm willing to receive You as my Saviour and trust You as my hope for Heaven.' That minute He will write P-a-i-d on your record and your record will be taken and thrown behind the back of God and will be as clean as that paper. Isn't that wonderful? That is the way your record will look.

"Now, let me ask you this: You realize you are a sinner; you realize that if you died today you would go to Hell; you realize that Jesus suffered Hell for you. Do you believe that if we knelt here right now and asked God's forgiveness and you put your faith in Christ, God would save you?"

"Yes, sir."

"Our Father, here is a man who needs to be saved. Jesus died for him. Lord, You have led me here today, and I thank You for it. Now may this be the greatest day in his life as he receives Jesus as Saviour. . . .

"Mr. Doe, while our heads are bowed, I'm going to ask you to do the finest thing you have ever done, and that is to just ask God to have mercy on you and save you. Would you do it in your own words? Just like you would talk to me, go ahead and talk to Him."

"Lord, I've sinned and I want You to forgive me. I want You to save me from my sins and I'll take You as my Saviour."

"Mr. Doe, while our heads are bowed, if you meant what you just said and you are willing today to give your life to Christ and trust Him as your hope for Heaven and you will make this the day of your acceptance of God's plan of salvation, would you take my hand as a token of it?" (That is one of the sweetest things. Their eyes are closed and lot of times they miss and they feel for your hand.)

Then you say, "Dear Lord, thank You that this man has trusted Jesus. And if the Bible is true and he has been sincere, he is Your child. Help him to see it now. In Jesus' name. Amen.

"God bless you, brother. Let me ask you this question now: According to this Book, where would you go if you died right now?"

"To Heaven."

"Do you believe this Book? When you get to the judgment seat, are you willing to trust your eternity on what this Book says?"

"Yes, sir."

"That means you are God's child. Now, suppose somebody asks you tomorrow, Mr. Doe, 'Are you a Christian?' — what are you going to tell them?"

"I'll tell them yes."

"If somebody says, 'When did you become a Christian?' — what are you going to tell them?"

"Yesterday."

May God use this simple plan to help make you a soul winner.

4
Let's Go Soul Winning In Public Places

Previously we have discussed at length witnessing in the home, preparation, etc. However, much effective soul winning can be done witnessing in public places. In this chapter we will deal basically with what might be called, "On the spot witnessing, casual witnessing."

1.   Places to Witness
Of course, a Christian should witness everywhere. To be the right kind of Christian I guess we should be willing to speak to anyone about the Saviour. Following is listed a few places where successful witnessing can be done.

Busses, planes, trains, etc. While riding on public transportation facilities is a good time to witness. I have won people to Christ on trains, busses, planes, cars, and other places such as these. Usually there is time for conversation. It is good perhaps to start the conversation about something besides Christianity or even religion. Perhaps ask the person about his life, his business, his home. Let him speak of his own interests for a while. Then gradually he will become interested in your interests and will ask you a few questions, whereupon you will have a good chance to present the Gospel to him. One reason to let him talk first is to enable you to find the best way to approach him.

Place of business. In places where the conversation and time are limited, a Gospel tract is in order. Places such as the grocery store, drug store, etc., would be included here, especially when the building is crowded and there is not sufficient time to explain salvation. Other places where soul winning can be done would be while getting a shoe shine, a haircut, etc. Many times I have won the shoeshine boy.

One time in Hearne, Texas, I won the shoeshine boy and got so excited that I forgot to pay him. He got so excited he forgot to ask for the money. When I got home I realized that I had not paid him, returned to the place and he was delighted as I gave him a dollar and apologized.

While I was pastor of the Miller Road Baptist Church in Garland, Texas, I went to get a shoeshine. Just about the time I had gotten courage enough to witness to the shine boy, he looked up at me and asked, "Sir, are you a Christian?" I was shocked that he had beat me to the question. I answered, "Yes, I am; are you?" He replied, "Yes, I was saved about five minutes ago. One of those Miller Road Baptist Church members came in and won me to the Lord Jesus and told me to witness to everybody." A simple word, "Are you a Christian?" "Have you ever been saved?" "Do you know Jesus?" "Do you know if you died that you could go to Heaven?" could set a person to thinking about his soul.

Hotel lobbies. Many times in hotel lobbies people are loitering and eager to talk. During a conference in Houston, Texas, several years ago I returned to my motel room only to find the door open and hear a noise. The noise seemed to originate in the bathroom. I inquired as to who was there and the colored maid answered that she was cleaning out the bathtub. I started to leave the room and wait until she finished, then decided to return and witness to her. So while she was cleaning out the tub, I told her about Jesus. She knelt right in the bathtub and received the Saviour and we had a shouting, old-fashioned time in the Lord. One never knows where he will meet a seeking sinner.

Bus stations, airports, train terminals. Once again here people are idle. Perhaps a good way would be to buy a newspaper, sit down beside someone as if you were taking a trip yourself. Begin talking about the war situation, or the time of day, or the weather, or ask where they are going, and let the conversation lead into a topic about the Lord Jesus Christ. In conferences around the country with Dr. John R. Rice, Dr. Tom Malone and others, we have seen scores of people saved in places such as these.

Other places to witness are washaterias, parks, or any other place where people are idle and have a few minutes to talk.

While a pastor in Texas we had a group of men who witnessed on the streets. Also, they went to the fairgrounds during the fair. They would put tracts in the cars in the parking lot during football games. Some wonderful experiences have come from this type of witnessing. Many of them would even go to taverns, and night clubs, stand on the outside and pass out tracts to people as they entered and left. One time our young people got burdened about souls, so spent most of the week on the city square witnessing to everyone who walked by. One young man won thirty-five souls in one week. One of our men won 169 souls in six months on the streets. Another won four or five every week to Jesus just witnessing on the streets.

Shopping centers. We have used what we call "Tract teams" to go to shopping centers to pass out tracts on a certain week night. In a new shopping center in Dallas, Texas, one of our men was passing out tracts. The shoppers seemed to think he was giving away chances on something. He did not tell them differently. A line formed. One man screamed from the rear, "What is this chance on?" Whereupon the soul

winner replied, "This is not a chance; this is a sure thing."
Another cried, "What are you giving away?" The answer was,
"A free home." The line grew until it was about a block
long. The man gave out all of his tracts and walked away
as the people found out how they could get a free home in
Heaven eternally.

Anytime you do a good deed is a good time to witness. Be
on the lookout for people who have cars that need pushing,
people whom you can help across the street, etc. After you
do a good deed for a person, he will sometimes feel obligated
to listen to what you have to say. This will give you an open
door to witness.

2. How to Witness Publicly

The method that we're going to mention can be used on
those in the homes who will not hear the complete plan;
those who are busy but nice; those whom you meet in passing. Also, it may be used on those to whom you witness in
public.

Simply ask, "Are you a Christian?"

*If they are not a Christian, ask them if they would like
to be.*

*If they show any sign at all of wanting to be saved, ask
them the following questions:*

Do you know that you are a sinner according to Romans
3:10 which says, "As it is written, There is none righteous,
no, not one," and Romans 3:23 which says, "For all have
sinned, and come short of the glory of God"?

Do you realize that all people who die in their sins must
pay the penalty for sin, which is eternal separation from
God as mentioned in Romans 5:12, "Wherefore, as by one
man sin entered into the world, and death by sin; and so
death passed upon all men, for that all have sinned," and in
Romans 6:23 where it says, "For the wages of sin is death;

but the gift of God is eternal life through Jesus Christ our Lord"? Do you understand that?

Do you realize that Jesus has paid the penalty for your sins and suffered the price for your sins on the cross according to Romans 5:8, which says, "But God commendeth his love toward us, in that, while we were yet sinners, Christ died for us"?

If their answers have been in the affirmative thus far, you may ask, "Do you believe if you bow your head now, simply asking God to forgive and save you, putting your faith and trust in Jesus to take you to Heaven, that He would save you?"

If they answer "Yes" to this question, ask them if you may pray. Pray very briefly since you are in public. A prayer like this will be sufficient: "Dear Lord, help this person to be saved today and to know that if he died, he would go to Heaven." Once again do not say "Amen" or let them know that you are ending the prayer. Stop the prayer abruptly.

Ask them to repeat a prayer after you. Once again you may use the sinner's prayer, "God be merciful to me a sinner and save my soul . . . I do now receive Jesus as my Saviour and trust Him to take me to Heaven when I die.

Ask them if they will receive Christ and mean it, to take you by the hand. Remember that you are in a hurry, that you are in a public place, and it may be embarrassing.

Get a quick promise from them to go to some church and make a public profession. Explain to them briefly what a public profession is. Some people will not understand. If you know of a church in the area, contact the pastor and let him visit the home. If you live in the area, you go to see them at their home at a later date. Do the best you can to get them to attend church the next Sunday.

If you are not successful in leading them to Christ, use some good Gospel tract. Leave it with them and ask them if they would read it when you are gone. Most people will do this.

You might even give them a New Testament. Mark a few Scriptures and ask them to read the Scriptures after you are gone.

Always keep your tracts clean and neat. Try to keep the corners from turning yellow or brown. Be sure they're kept in a good place so that they will be as attractive as possible when given out. Tracts have a tremendous ministry when used properly. We have received tracts from all over America.

One young lady was leaving home. She had separated from her husband and was leaving home on a train. One of our college students was returning to college after the holidays at home and was passing out tracts on the train. The young lady received a tract, was saved, returned home and was reconciled to her husband.

A young man on a ship in Japan received one of our tracts from his mother. He was saved, won fifteen of his buddies to Jesus, started a prayer meeting, Sunday School and preaching service on the ship, all because of one tract.

One of our ladies was passing out tracts at a bus station. A man on his way to prison was handed one. He was saved on his way to prison, wrote us a letter about it. Within two years he came to our church, was baptized and publicly thanked the lady who gave him the tract at the bus station two years before.

Just a few days before writing this chapter we received two tracts from people who had been saved simply through the tract ministry.

When witnessing in public, do not be intimidated. The natural tendency is for us to be embarrassed a bit. Quickly control the conversation; speak to each one around about Jesus; and make the atmosphere controlled by your conversation rather than your being intimidated by theirs. In other words, make them feel like a fool instead of you.

You cannot press long for a decision in public. If the decision cannot be made, simply give a tract.

Casually get their name and address and write it down. You may either contact the pastor who lives near them, or some soul winner in their area. If this is not possible, you may send them some good literature or some good Gospel paper that will lead them to Christ later.

Remember always to be courteous. There is never a time for a soul winner to be ugly, unkind, or discourteous. You are God's representative; be the best one that you can be.

5
Let's Go Soul Winning In the Hospital

One of the finest times to reach people for Jesus is in times of illness, bereavement, etc. For example, I have found it wise to give an invitation at a funeral. This is never an invitation to walk the aisle but an invitation to raise the hand if willing to accept Christ. Every advantage should be taken to win people to Christ. At a wedding rehearsal, if there are strangers, an invitation can be given very successfully. Many have been saved at weddings and funerals.

Recently while on a visit in Texas a lady reminded me of the conversion of her father. Her brother had been killed in a car wreck. I preached his funeral in Sulphur Springs, Texas, and gave the invitation. Her father ran down the aisle, threw himself over the body of his son, and was gloriously converted. The next Sunday he walked the aisle in a church in that area and became very shortly the chairman of the board and the Sunday School superintendent. He recently passed away and has gone to be with his son and with his Saviour in Heaven.

Another time it was my joy to lead a father to Christ over

the casket of his little six-month-old baby. In one service I was conducting the funeral for a man who had influence with Little League ball players. Nine ball players were saved in one funeral service. In visiting the home before a funeral we have had many saved. One day there were six saved in one home. Just recently here in Hammond, a seventy-three-year-old man was won to Christ in the home of his brother who had lost his wife.

One of the finest places to win people is in the hospital. Notice a few things we will mention concerning hospital soul winning and visitation.

An early visit is certainly in order. This is especially true for pastors who are allowed to visit at any time of the day. I find a visit around six in the morning or seven in the morning is a good time. There is not much activity and the person is usually alert and ready to listen. It also does not interfere with his day. This is especially good as many operations are early in the morning and the person can be talked to before surgery.

Be brief. Usually it is best to quote the Scripture rather than showing it to them, and the shorter plan is much better. Many reasons could be given for this: (1) The people do not feel well and a lengthy conversation might impair their health. (2) Usually you can build a better reputation at the hospital and have better relations with the hospital attendants if you are brief.

Use tracts. The people have time to read, and reading material is always valued.

Witness to those in other beds. It has been my policy through the years to try to witness to every person in the room with the patient I am visiting. "How are you feeling today?" or "Do you plan to go home soon?" or some other statement can lead to a conversation about Jesus. Literally hundreds have been won in my ministry by this method. Some are in Heaven now. Others have been healed and are making good members of Bible-preaching churches.

Always witness to a lost person just before surgery. This is a time when one certainly needs the Lord and would be receptive to your ministry of prayer and witnessing.

Always witness to visitors and relatives in the room. Remember, they too have tender hearts and the Lord may be using this time to lead them to Himself.

Whether you win them or not, always have a prayer of faith for them before you leave. Pray for their recovery; pray for God's blessings upon them; pray for courage and strength and faith.

Always let them talk to you a while about their condition. This will open the door for you to talk to them about their spiritual condition.

Report to them about the church services. If they are members of your church or if they attend, you may want to take them a church bulletin. If there is revival going on, you may want to take the evangelist by to visit them. Some people even take tapes of sermons and recording machines so they can hear the sermon of last Sunday.

Always observe the rules of the hospital. Remember you are a guest of the hospital and you are planting seed for future opportunities. Do not be obnoxious or intrusive. Be careful to observe all the rules.

Buy numbers of get-well cards and send them to lost people in hospitals. For that matter, send them to saved people too, but receiving a get-well card from you will certainly open some doors for your witnessing to them in the future.

Recently a lost man in our city was ill and he required surgery. Every week I sent him a get-well card. When I came by to visit him, he began to weep and said, "You were the only person who sent me a card." I immediately led him to Christ, turned to his wife and she was saved. Within a few weeks they had walked the aisle and made public their profession of faith in our church.

It has been my policy for a long while to send get-well cards to everyone I know in any hospital, whether church members or not.

6
Let's Visit an Absentee

One of the problems that every preacher and Christian worker faces is keeping the members faithful and contacting them when they are absent. We're constantly reminding the Sunday School teachers to visit absentees and get them back in class, and let them know they're welcome. A few of the things we have found through the years to be helpful concerning this matter are as follows:

The most important absentee to visit is the one who was absent last Sunday. Nothing should be taken for granted here. Every member of the church is a potential backslider. Just as one drink can lead to drunkenness, and one evil thought can lead to adultery, even so can one absence lead to backsliding. To be sure, all absentees should be visited, but it is tremendously important that a person get a visit the first Sunday he is absent.

So many churches have tried the plan of a post card the first week, a phone call the second week, and a visit the third. This should be reversed. Do all you can to get him back the first Sunday. After three weeks he is a habitual absentee and is out of the habit of coming. Again, I say, the most important absentee to visit is the one who was absent last Sunday.

Make a list of absentees every week for every worker. We must be careful not to drop names too hurriedly from our Sunday School rolls. The easiest thing in the world to join should be a Sunday School. The hardest thing to quit should be the Sunday School. Pupils should not be dropped unless they die, move, or run off. If we take a member off our rolls, we will forget them and they will not be visited as absentees. Some churches find it advisable to have an active and inactive roll. This is well and good, if the inactive roll is visited as well as the active roll.

The Seven-Up Club. We have found it advisable to have what we call a Seven-Up Club. This is composed of all the people in our church who will promise to visit at least three prospects a week and four absentees a week or more, making a total of seven or up. The cards may be given out on Wednesday evening. They may be kept until the next Wednesday, turned in with the results of the visit. This insures the person of making at least seven visits a week for the Lord.

When making an absentee visit, make it more casual than a prospect visit. This is especially true if you know the absentee personally, and in most cases you will. The visit can be folksy and conversational and can make for the class members to get to know each other better.

Stress what they missed last Sunday. So many absentee visitors emphasize how much they missed the absentee. This is well and good, but the thing that should be stressed the most is how much they missed. Tell them what a good service you had Sunday. Tell them how many conversions the church had. Tell them about the music, the good sermon, etc. In other words, create in them a desire to want to come back next week.

Do not talk about their being absent last Sunday but rather their being present this Sunday. Say very little concerning their absence. Scolding would not be in order, but rather get them promised for next Sunday.

Remember the advantages of absentee visitation. First, it gives the teacher the need of the pupil. No person can be the proper kind of teacher unless he knows the needs of his pupils. These needs cannot be known properly unless the teacher has been in the home of the pupil. To learn about the parents, the environment, the house, etc., is important for the teacher to do the most good for the pupil.

In the second place, it lets the pupils know the teacher. It is always good for the pupil to be able to see the teacher outside the Sunday School class and to become somewhat of a pal and a buddy with the teacher. This is aided by a personal visit to the home.

In the third place, absentee visitation also aids in lesson preparation. Knowing the condition of the pupil's home will enable the teacher to include the necessary thoughts and observations in his lesson on Sunday. This is tremendously important.

Always have a prayer in the home before leaving. Many boys and girls (and adults for that matter) never pray at home. The Sunday School teacher can bring a little bit of Heaven into the home if he will offer a prayer before leaving. This is tremendously important in an absentee visitation.

7
Let's Have a
Public Invitation

After observing for nearly fifteen years the preaching of hundreds of preachers across America, I have come to the conclusion that many of us need intensive help in the conducting of a public invitation. Many wonderful Gospel messages can be rendered ineffective by a weak invitation. On the other hand, many average preachers can be rewarded greatly with the use of an effective, pungent public invitation. Though in many places a public invitation is seldom used and even considered out of date, it is still true that the greatest soul winning churches utilize an effective spiritual, Spirit-filled, powerful invitation as their greatest means of evangelism. May we look at a few practical pointers concerning the invitation.

1. Starting the Invitation

Do not reveal the closing of the sermon. When the sermon reaches a high point or a climax, then would be a good time to close abruptly! Even if the sermon is not completed, sometimes God may lead one to close prematurely in order to start the invitation from a high spiritual plane. This also prevents the unsaved from digging in, so to speak, before the invitation is given.

Upon the completion of the sermon, ask the people to bow their heads and close their eyes. Such statements as these are sometimes effective, "Every head bowed, every eye closed; no one is leaving, no one is moving while God speaks to our hearts."

Now ask the congregation with heads bowed, "How many can say under God that I know that if I died momentarily I would go to Heaven?" Such an approach may be used, "Now while every head is bowed, every eye is closed, no one is leaving, no one is moving, with God being our witness, those of you who can say, 'If I died today I know beyond any shadow of doubt that I would go to Heaven,' would you raise your hand?"

Ask lost people to raise their hands. A good way would be as follows, "Now while our heads are bowed, some of you could not raise your hands that you know that if you died today you would go to Heaven. You were too honest to raise your hand; you were sincere in not raising your hand, but would you say, 'Preacher, I want to know that I am saved. I wish I could say that if I died now I would go to Heaven.

I want to know that I'm a Christian. Please pray for me'? If you can say that while everyone is still and no one is looking; if you want me to pray that you may know that if you died you would go to Heaven, would you lift your hand?" While the hands are being lifted, you may simply acknowledge each hand raised with a "God bless you" or, "I see you" or "I'll pray for you" or some other acknowledgement.

While heads are still bowed, pray for them. Such a prayer as this would be fine: "Dear Lord, help the people who raised their hands to receive Christ today. May this be the biggest day in their lives and may today they have the joy of knowing that if they died they would go to Heaven. Bless the lady on the aisle near the front; bless the man in the rear of the balcony. I pray that You would save those two on my left, and the one in the back at the right of the auditorium. Speak to their hearts and may today be the biggest day of their lives as they receive Jesus as their Saviour." At the conclusion of this prayer, do not give away the closing of the prayer and do not say "Amen," but continue speaking.

Lead them to pray silently where they are sitting, thusly: "Now while our heads are bowed; you raised your hand, you said that you wanted to know that if you died today you would go to Heaven. You can know; the Bible tells of a man who prayed the sinner's prayer and put his faith in the Saviour. Would you right now simply pray silently this prayer, 'Dear Lord, be merciful to me a sinner and save me now. I do now receive Jesus as my Saviour from sin and trust Him to take me to Heaven when I die' "? Insist that they pray this prayer silently. You may even quote the prayer again to them.

2. The Public Profession

Lead them to a public profession in the service. Tell them exactly what they are to do. For example, "Now while every head is bowed and every eye is closed, you have raised your hand to admit your lost condition, you have said that you wanted to know that if you died you would go to Heaven. If you would make this the day of your acceptance of Christ and make this the red letter day of your life by receiving Jesus as your Saviour I'm going to ask you to do this: We're going to stand and sing in a minute; as we stand and sing I'm going to ask you to leave your seat, come to the nearest aisle, walk down that aisle to the altar and have a seat on the front row and let me tell the people that you are receiving Christ as your Saviour today. I beg you in Jesus' name do not let Satan win the battle. Leave your seat when we sing;

come to the aisle, down to the front, and let me tell the people that you are receiving Christ today."

Start the invitation hymn. Have the people stand. Have the choir lead the song militantly. This song should have been previously practiced by the choir. It should be rendered as a special number. It should not be dragged and it should not be whiny. It should be a real good musical presentation. At our services we always use the same song to open every invitation. "Just As I Am" is the song.

Continue singing the same song as long as folks are coming. As long as people are walking the aisle, it is not good to change the song. If God is blessing a certain invitation song we often sing it four or five times all the way through. As soon as people quit coming on one song, it is good to change songs.

Let the people observe the invitation as long as folks are coming. If the invitation begins successfully and people are walking the aisle, it is good usually to let the congregation observe it. This will be a blessing to others and perhaps other lost ones can be won as they see people walking the aisle. As soon as people quit walking the aisle or if the invitation starts slowly, I would suggest an early time of asking the people to bow their heads in prayer. Once again, I would make an appeal of urgency and continue singing with heads bowed.

The pastor should control the invitation. We have found it advantageous for the pastor to decide when the songs should be sung. For example, the pastor may, by the lifting of his hand, stop the choir; ask the people to bow their heads and say words such as this: "Now while our heads are bowed would you come; God loves you; Jesus wants to save you. This could be the greatest day in your life. As the choir sings 'Softly and Tenderly Jesus Is Calling' would you leave your seat, come down the aisle and receive Christ as your Saviour? Do not linger; today is your opportunity." By that time the choir will have found the next song and can begin singing. Have the choir trained so that the rustling of pages will not interfere. Any moving on the part of the people or the choir can be a hindrance to an invitation. It is never good for the song leader, a few minutes before the end of the sermon, to turn to the choir and have them find the song as the pastor closes his message. The closer the message gets to the end and the farther toward the invitation and into the invitation the pastor gets, the quieter the service should be. Also, the pastor should control the loudness or softness of the song. Our choir director is trained to sing the song loudly and at an average tempo unless otherwise directed by the pastor. The pastor may say, "While our heads are bowed, the choir will sing softly the next stanza" or he may say, "As our heads are bowed and God is working, the choir will sing softly and slowly their next stanza." In other words, the changes of songs, tempo, volume, etc., during the invitation, should be controlled by the pastor.

Have soul winners at the altar to kneel with those who come forward. Many people come down the aisles in our churches under conviction who never get converted. They need to be shown the Scriptures, prayed with at the altar, and led to Christ in the service. We have some people trained to do this. The pastor may simply motion for a soul winner as he sees the person coming forward. The soul winner may kneel at the altar or have a seat on the front row and deal with them. It is our opinion that it is much better to deal with people in the service than to take them out of the service. The inspiration is there, the singing is there, and we find it better to leave them in the service until its completion. After the soul winner is satisfied, he may lead the convert to a seat on the front and introduce the convert to the church clerk or secretary who in turn will take his name and give it to the pastor.

3.   Make Much of Those Saved

The pastor then may read to the people the names of those coming. This is a very important time. It should not be done quickly. Each person should be presented to the people, asked to stand at the front, and the pastor should say some sweet word of encouragement and blessing to the people concerning the convert. Remember, a new name has just been written down in Heaven. Hell has been robbed; Heaven has been populated; Christ has seen the travail of His soul and been satisfied. Heaven is rejoicing, and the angels are shouting. We, too, should make much over people saved in our services.

Have relatives and friends come to the altar and stand beside loved ones. One of the most blessed parts of our service is the time when mothers and fathers come and stand at the altar beside children, husbands come and join wives, wives come to rejoice with husbands, and friends rejoice with friends who have been saved in the service. Some time you may ask a husband to kiss his wife, or a loved one to testify. Usually there is weeping and rejoicing at the altar, and the entire congregation can share in this rejoicing.

After the names are read and the people are lined up across the front, suggest that the membership come by after the benediction and shake hands with the new converts, encouraging them and welcoming them to the body of Christ. This, too, can be a time of real blessing as the people share in the wonderful experience.

In the benediction, the pastor could pray for the converts. In other words, as the pastor leads the closing prayer he could say, "Dear Lord, bless Johnny who has been saved today. Help him to grow up to be a fine Christian man. Bless Mr. Jones who has been saved. We pray that he will be the kind of Christian You would want him to be. We're thankful that Mrs. Johnson has been saved, and that Mr.

Williams has found the Lord. We pray that You will bless Susie, Mary, Bill and the others, and grant, dear Lord, that they will be great Christians." In other words, in closing have a prayer for God to bless the converts.

This is not the only way, of course, to conduct an invitation. It may not even be the best way. To be sure, there are many other good ways. But this pastor has found through fifteen years' experience that this is the most profitable way for his ministry. Perhaps, some of the aforementioned suggestions will help others in inviting the unsaved to come to the Saviour. One thing for sure: we need to put more emphasis upon the public invitation in our churches. May God help us to realize that this is a life or death proposition. Eternity is at stake. Eternal values rest on our efficiency and the anointing of God upon our methods and upon our message. May we spend more time than the surgeon would spend, and be more diligent than the doctor would be as we wrestle, operate and work with the immortal souls of men, women, boys and girls.

8
Let's Witness During the Invitation

Much has been said pro and con about witnessing during an invitation. By this we mean going to someone in the service who has not come forward and encouraging him to step out and receive Christ as Saviour. Much harm can be done here, however. As is always the case when much harm can be done, much good can be done also. If done properly, it can be a blessing in a church service. Many of the greatest soul-winning churches in America have people trained to speak a word of encouragement to the unsaved who do not come forward on their own volition during the invitation. Let us look at a few suggestions concerning this important phase of the invitation and of soul winning.

If you know someone who is lost, sit with that person or near him during the service. To be sure there will be times when God will lead you to walk across the auditorium or even from the choir to deal with an unsaved person. This will be the exception, however, rather than the rule. It is always best to sit near the person so as to be able to talk to him with as little embarrassment as possible. Much harm has been done by unwise witnessing because of improper planning and preparation.

Be sure that your body is clean. Close contact is necessary in this kind of witnessing. Hence, we should avoid odors such as body and breath.

It is usually best to wait until heads are bowed. Most pastors sometime in an invitation will ask the people to bow their heads and close their eyes. This is the best time to do personal work. The people will not see you coming to them. You will not interrupt the service and it will not be embarrassing for them when you come. Pastors should remember to give their people an opportunity by asking for bowed heads sometime during the invitation. This will encourage Christians to do soul winning in the invitation time. Usually when people are not looking, a convert is much more receptive, less embarrassed and much more likely to make a decision for Christ. If he does not make his decision, at least he will be more likely to come back again to visit if he knows he has not been publicly embarrassed.

Do not ramble around promiscuously. Much danger is done by over-zealous people who tend to embarrass the church members by asking them if they are saved. Just because you do not know someone does not mean they are lost. Of course, in rare cases the Spirit of God may lead one to a complete stranger. If the Lord leads, follow. Much care, however, should be taken in this matter. I have known people to just walk up and down the aisles asking everyone who looked a little bit solemn if they were saved. This is usually not a good procedure.

Come to him from the rear. If a person is sitting on the left side of the building, it would be wise for the soul winner to go up the aisle on the right side until he is at the back of the auditorium. Then approach the person from the rear. This will give him an element of surprise and prevent him from becoming offended before you talk to him.

Introduce yourself graciously. Words such as, "How do you do; my name is Smith. We're so happy to have you in the service today and I trust that you have received a blessing. . . . What is your name, please sir? . . . Well, I'm so glad to know you, Mr. Jones, and I was wondering if you know you are a Christian." If the answer is "No" to this, then of course the green light is on.

Ask him if he would like to be a Christian. Such words as this would be in order. "Mr. Jones, the greatest thing in the world is to know that if you died you would go to Heaven. Wouldn't you like to have that peace today?"

If he says he would, suggest he come to the altar with you and tell the pastor. Words such as this could be used. "Mr. Jones, I'm so glad that you want to be a Christian. If you would receive Christ as your Saviour today, come with me to the altar and let the pastor rejoice in your decision."

Sometimes he will not come. In that case you may simply say, "Mr. Jones, could I have a prayer with you here at your seat that you will receive Christ as your Saviour?" If this is permissible, have a brief prayer such as mentioned in the previous chapter concerning dealing with people at the altar. You may pray thusly, "Dear Lord, we're glad that Mr. Jones has come today. We're glad to have him. We pray that You will bless his heart in the service and grant that he will be saved today. May this service be the greatest service in his life and may he receive Jesus as Saviour today."

Close the prayer abruptly. Ask him if he would pray. A prayer such as, "Now, Mr. Jones, while our heads are bowed, our eyes are closed, would you be willing now to ask God to have mercy on you and make you His child today? Go ahead and say, 'Lord, be merciful to me a sinner . . . forgive my sins . . . and save me this morning . . . I do now receive Jesus as my Saviour . . . and trust Him to take me to Heaven when I die. . . .'"

Ask him to take your hand if he is receiving Christ. The conversation would go something like this: "Mr. Jones, while our heads are bowed and our eyes are closed, I'm so happy that you have come to Christ today. If you meant your prayer and would make this the day of your trusting Jesus, as a token of it, would you please take my hand?"

After he takes your hand, you pray again. In your prayer thank the Lord that Mr. Jones has been saved and pray for God's blessings upon him. Make this prayer very brief.

Now ask him if he will go to the altar with you and tell the preacher that he has trusted Jesus. Words like this could be used: "Now, Mr. Jones, let's go to the altar and tell the preacher that you've trusted Jesus." Then look at Mrs. Jones or a child or a friend and ask one of them if they will come with him to the altar. Of course they will, whereupon you can take Mr. Jones to the altar, introduce him to the pastor, explain to him that Mr. Jones has been saved in the service, and he can rejoice with you over Mr. Jones' decision.

9

Let's Win a Soul At the Altar

As mentioned in the previous chapter, we have found it advisable to have soul winners trained to work with people who come forward in the services. This should be an art. These people should be well trained, well instructed, well disciplined and anointed people. Following are some suggestions concerning dealing with people at the altar. Bear in mind, these suggestions are to be used in the helping of people who have been convicted in the services, who have come forward at the invitation to receive Christ as Saviour.

1. Step-by-Step Instructions

Be clean bodily. No other place will require more intimate contact in soul winning than at the altar. If you plan to do any soul winning at the altar, be sure that your body is clean, that necessary deodorant has been used so as not to offend.

Keep breath freshener handy. At the conclusion of the service, and just before the invitation song, place a mint in your mouth or some other kind of breath freshener. Due to the singing and the noise of the service, you will be talking in close contact to the inquirer. Do not be offensive in any way, especially concerning your breath.

Introduce yourself and speak a word of greeting. For example, the pastor has called you and said, "Mr. Jones, Mr. Smith here wants to come to Christ. Would you pray with him about the matter?" Immediately you should introduce yourself to the seeker such as, "My name is Smith. I'm so glad you're coming today. My heart is made happy when anyone comes to Jesus Christ. Shall we kneel here please and notice some Scriptures in the Bible?" In some places it is better to have a seat on the front. In the case of a small altar in the church, or not much distance between the front row and the pulpit, or in other circumstances that would prevent kneeling, it would be wise to have a seat on the front. You could say simply, "May we have a seat on the front?"

Read to him Romans 10:9-13. Keep this marked in your Bible and keep a marker at the right page so you can turn to it readily. There is not much time to use a great deal of Scripture. These Scriptures are very inclusive and can be used of God to win a soul any place, especially at the altar. Read Romans 10:9-13 to them, with special emphasis on verse 13.

Ask this question, "Do you realize that you are a sinner?"

Now ask, "Do you realize that people who die in their sins must go to Hell when they die?"

Ask, "Do you believe that Jesus Christ on the cross paid your penalty for sin, to keep you from going to Hell?"

Ask this question, "Do you believe, knowing this, that if you were to call upon Him now to save you and trust Him with all of your heart as your Saviour, He would make you His child?"

Suggest they bow their head with you for prayer, if ALL the previous questions have been answered in the affirmative. You may use words such as these, "Now would you bow your head with me and let me pray that God will make you His child today?"

As you bow your head to pray, ask him to place his hand on Romans 10:9-13. Read it to him again and then begin to pray.

Pray briefly. Pray simply. Do not pray such a pretty prayer that his will seem out of place. A prayer such as this would be in order, "Dear Lord, thank You that Mr. Jones wants to come to Christ today and I pray that today he will receive the Saviour and know in his heart that he is Your child. Help him now, Lord. Give him faith to believe, and may this be the day of his conversion. . . ." Do not say "Amen" at the close of the prayer or "in Jesus' name." Stop abruptly and say, "Let's keep our heads bowed and our eyes closed. . . ."

Lead him to pray. At the altar usually it is best to tell him what to pray; sometimes in certain conditions you will simply tell him about what to pray. For example, "Now while our heads are bowed, Mr. Jones, and our eyes are closed, would you be willing to ask God now to forgive your sins and tell Him that you do want to receive Jesus as your Saviour? Go ahead and try out loud; ask Him to forgive you and save you." If Mr. Jones does not seem to be able to pray his own prayer, you may ask him to repeat after you a prayer such as, "Mr. Jones, while our heads are bowed and our eyes are closed, would you out loud say this prayer and mean it, 'Dear Lord, be merciful to me a sinner . . . and save me now . . . I do now receive Jesus . . . as my Saviour . . . and trust Him to take me to Heaven when I die' "? You may want to use another type prayer, but be sure that your heart is in it and that God burdens you to where it will not simply be a rote proposition but a sincerity in your heart and the heart of the seeker.

Now say approximately the following words, "Now while our heads are bowed and our eyes are closed, Mr. Jones, if you meant your prayer and if you today are receiving Christ as your Saviour, if you're making this the moment of your salvation, would you be willing, man to man, to place your hand in mine?" The seeker takes your hand, then you say, "God bless you!" After he takes your hand, and while your heads are still bowed, you pray a prayer of thanksgiving something like this: "Dear Lord, thank You today that Mr. Jones has received the Saviour. Thank You that he has trusted Jesus. And if he has been sincere and if Your Word is true, he is Your child and if he died now, he would go to Heaven. God bless him now and give him peace and assurance. In Jesus' name. Amen."

Now ask him, "Mr. Jones, according to the Bible, where would you go if you died now?" Usually by now in a public service he is very pleased and satisfied that he is God's child and has become a new creature.

Lead Mr. Jones to the church clerk or secretary. Explain to her that he has been converted. She will take his name and address and give it to the pastor.

2.   Some Dont's of Working at the Altar

Do not spend too much time. Bear in mind that the average invitation is ten or fifteen minutes at the most. Also, the person has already heard the Gospel in the sermon and has responded to this message. He simply needs to be handled carefully so as to have assurance of salvation.

Don't use too many Scriptures. This may be done later on in the home as you help them know the Word of God more perfectly, or can be done after the service in a private meeting. But simply the minimum of Scriptures should be used at the altar.

Don't stay at the altar if not having success. If the person has a hard time getting assurance, lead him to a side room or ask the pastor to help some way. Do not linger and prolong the service unduly, if the person is unwilling or unable to have assurance. It is tragic that many people come to the altars of our churches and are not dealt with properly.

Of course, these are not the only suggestions. No doubt, there are some better ones and some just as good. But one thing for sure: we need to spend more time and be more careful in dealing with people at the altar. Remember that "faith cometh by hearing, and hearing by the word of God." When people walk the aisles of our churches, they are our obligation and our responsibility. May God help us to carry the weight of the burden of the service.

Sunday morning and Sunday night is more than just a time of worship. It is more than just a time of fellowship. It is more than just a time of getting together and seeing how the friends and neighbors are. It is a time of eternity for lost people. A time to break our hearts to reach them. A time to lead us to do our best to get everyone saved possible and to lead those who come to Christ to real definite assurance. This can be done with the proper burden and the proper emphasis at the altar. May God help us to do it wisely.

3. Coming by Membership

In the invitation there are people, of course, coming to present themselves for membership in the church. Some churches vote on them immediately at the altar. Others wait until the end of the month, at the regular church business meeting. In either case there are people month by month walking the aisles wanting to unite with our churches. There are several suggestions that should be helpful in the handling of these people in the invitation also.

The pastor should welcome them graciously, expressing joy at their coming.

He may then introduce them to one of the personal workers at the altar. If the pastor feels it necessary, he may ask the personal workers to have a prayer of thanksgiving with them for their coming. Sometimes it might be advisable to have a prayer of dedication and ask them to pray also. Usually this is not best.

The personal worker may then introduce himself and speak delight at their coming.

Then the personal worker may then introduce them to the church clerk who, in turn, takes their name, address, and necessary information.

These people should also have their names read. They should stand at the front and after the benediction be welcomed by the membership. It is always a big time when new members are added to the church family. Let us make it a blessed time of rejoicing with our people.

4. Dealing With a Child at the Altar

A word of caution about the handling of children at the altar. One of the best Scriptures that can be used for a child is Revelation 3:20. This deals with Jesus knocking at the door. You may remind the child the simplicity of inviting someone in who knocks at the door of his home. You may also remind him that Jesus is knocking at his heart's door and wants to enter. Ask him if he is willing to let Jesus come into his heart. If the answer is in the affirmative, then the head may be bowed and you may lead the child in the same type prayer mentioned previously in this chapter. After the child has been converted, he should go to his parents and explain to them his conversion, if they are in the service. Someone should come and stand with the child at the altar— his Sunday School teacher, a friend, his mother and father, a neighbor or if need be, a perfect stranger, if the others are not available. In other words, the child should have a big buddy at the altar.

10
Let's Make a Schedule

This article is written to the many thousands of good men across America and around the world who want to win souls and be what God wants them to be as pastors. After observing the lives of pastors through many years it has been my feeling that we do not discipline our lives enough, and the average pastor would do well to live more by schedule and less by chance. The word "discipline" comes from the word disciple; and so if we are to be a disciple, we must be disciplined. If a preacher isn't careful he will let circumstances control his schedule rather than his schedule control the circumstances. Following are some suggestions to help us live a fuller life in the ministry.

1. Visit Hospitals in the Morning

It has been my policy for many years to visit with people just before surgery if at all possible. Since surgery is usually early in the morning, this necessitates getting to the hospital between six and seven o'clock. When I go to pray with someone just before surgery, naturally I find myself visiting the others in the hospital and making my regular rounds. From this beginning I have decided that the best time to visit the hospital is in the early morning hours. Usually people do not sleep late at the hospital, and around seven o'clock is a good time to visit them. This keeps the hospital visitation from interrupting the daily schedule and hurting the pastor's soul-winning ·time. House-to-house soul winning cannot be done at six o'clock in the morning. The hospital visiting can, leaving the other hours for soul winning, etc.

2.   Prayer Time Should Be All the Time

Of course, a preacher should have a private time of devotion every morning. There should be times of seasons of prayer — even praying into the night — but a preacher can take many advantages of prayer that will be helpful. When a letter is written or dictated, pray for the person to whom you are writing at the conclusion of the letter. When reading the day's mail, as you read each letter whisper a prayer for each person who wrote you. After a telephone conversation, ask God to bless the one to whom you just spoke. When company comes to the study or to the parsonage, have prayer with them before saying good-by. Of course, the pastor should have a family altar and grace at the table in addition to the other times of prayer. I have found it beneficial to keep a prayer list in my car, praying for people as I drive to and from work. A person could add as much as an hour a day to his prayer time if he would pray while driving. Then, of course, on Saturday evening there should be an intensity of prayer for the services on Sunday.

At our church we have a weekly deacons' prayer meeting on Saturday evening. On Saturday evening the pastor should pray in the pulpit. It has been my policy to drive around town and pray for the city; also to stop in front of the homes of unsaved people for whom I am concerned and pray for them on Saturday evening. If we would bathe our regular duties in prayer, it would help us to spend much more time in prayer.

For example, if I write ten lettters a day, talk on the telephone ten times a day, plus my other regular prayer time, I will have prayed over fifty different times each day beside my own regular private devotion time. May God help us preachers to learn to pray.

3. Studying for Sermons

One of the hardest things to do is to find a sermon when you are looking for one. For a preacher to come to Saturday night with no sermon for Sunday and to seek one is almost an impossibility. For a number of years I have given Wednesday afternoon to Bible study. Four hours of studying the Bible and preparing sermons. However, I do not seek sermons as I study. I think it is best to study for your own delight and personal knowledge of the Bible. As you come to a certain Scripture which looms out in your mind, outline it quickly. Put it in your file and keep it there. You will be surprised how much fresher the sermon will be if it is gotten out of a spontaneous thrill rather than a sense of duty in preparing the message. I have now in my files over eighty sermons outlined that I have never preached that have been prepared in this way. Of course, the preacher should study the Bible for his own private joy every day, but one afternoon a week definitely given to studying the Word of God would be beneficial, in addition to the daily study.

I have also placed in my car a little "Bread of Life" loaf with Scripture cards in it. I took the ash tray out of the car and the cards fit perfectly. That way I can memorize Scriptures as I drive down the street. On one recent trip to the airport I was able to memorize fifty verses. Once again, we have utilized time normally wasted.

4. Soul-Winning Time

Once again, to live by schedule is important. I have found through the years the wisdom of setting a certain time each week for soul-winning visitation. Of course, pastors should be constantly on the lookout for sinners. When salesmen come to see him, he should be a ready witness. In hospital visitation, counseling, weddings, funerals, etc., the pastor should be constantly trying to win people. But this is not enough. The successful soul-winning pastor should spend some definite hours planned each week on the field in house-to-house witnessing. I have utilized for many years Thursday afternoons from one to five, Friday afternoon from one to five, and several hours on Saturday for soul winning. Only for speaking engagements or funerals do I consider changing my schedule.

If the pastor would rigidly adhere to a certain period each week for soul winning it would certainly increase and revitalize his ministry. Most of us intend to win souls when we have time, but of course many duties of the pastor leave us little time.

Soul winning must be done on purpose. It must be planned like prayer meeting is planned; like Sunday School is planned; like the preaching service is planned. If a pastor would be as diligent in planning his soul-winning time as he is his other meetings, the other meetings would certainly take on new life.

5.   Counseling

Certainly a great part of the pastorate is counseling with people concerning problems. If the preacher isn't careful he will find himself spending most of his time as a marriage counselor, psychiatrist, etc., and find the rest of his schedule being built around the counseling. I have found it advantageous to counsel with people before and after the services on Sunday. Usually someone wants to see me after the Sunday morning service or the Sunday night service or before the Sunday evening service — also, after the Wednesday evening service.

For example, if a couple wants to get married and wants to plan the wedding, we do it after the service. This keeps much of the counseling from interfering with the pastor's regularly set schedule. Saturday morning is also a good time for counseling. It will not interfere with the Saturday afternoon visitation and will hardly interrupt the pastor's regular routine.

6. Time for the Family

Dr. Bob Jones, Sr., says, "Duties never conflict." One does not have to choose between being a good pastor and a good father, or a good pastor and a good husband; a good pastor and a good citizen. Duties do not conflict. In fact, a man cannot be a good pastor who is not a good husband and a good father. It is important that a pastor discipline his schedule so as to give some time weekly to his family life.

A number of suggestions are made in the chapter, "The Evangelistic Pastor and His Family." Some suggestions for this: (1) *Take time for meals with the family.* At our house through the years we have tried to take plenty of time to eat together. When one eats, we all eat. We schedule our meals; gather around the table and enjoy family life at the table. One of the tragedies in the home of the average pastor is the fact that the family seldom eats together.

(2) Another suggestion is that *the pastor go home for lunch.* Once again, this will give him time in the middle of the day with his family. It will not interfere with his regular schedule and will enable him to spend an hour or so with his wife and family.

(3) *Take the family out to eat periodically.* Perhaps, even once a week the family could go out to eat. This would not necessarily be expensive. A family could eat anywhere ranging from expensive steak to inexpensive hamburgers, but it is such a vital part in a family's life to eat together.

Not only is it important in the matter of meals but it is

very important that a pastor spend some time each week with his children. This time with the children should be just as much a part of the schedule as the Sunday morning service and visitation time. To the average pastor who is in town most of the time, a regular afternoon could be chosen. For many years I took the children on Tuesday afternoon for a get-together. Perhaps Saturday would be better for some. But half a day a week with the children should be a must in the schedule of a busy pastor.

Such places as the park, picnic, trip to the zoo, etc., will pay dividends in the lives of the children. The pastor should be a pal to his children and not only should spend some time with them collectively but with them individually.

When you run to the store, ask one of the children to go with you. As you go, make love to him. Spend some tender moments; counsel with him, etc. This time which is usually wasted can be used to be beneficial in the life of a busy pastor. Susannah Wesley with nineteen children gave each

child a private conference each week. For example, John Wesley had to spend time with his mother each Thursday evening learning about life and its problems.

Not only should a pastor spend time with his children, but he should spend some time with his wife. One of the most important things for a pastor is to stay in love with his wife and for them to continue to be sweethearts through their ministry. A pastor's heart should never grow cold toward his wife. He would do well to take time to go shopping with her; take her out to eat privately occasionally; go visiting with her, and other activities. Included in my schedule often is for my wife to make visits with me. We have had the joy of winning people together, visiting hospitals together, etc.

Not only should a pastor spend time with his children and his wife, but he should find time in his schedule to see that his wife gets to spend some time alone. The pastor could take an afternoon a week, for example, when he baby-sits and gives the wife the car. She can do her grocery shopping or can have the afternoon to herself. God bless the dear preachers' wives. Probably they are the most neglected people in the world. For years now I have taken a good part of Saturday afternoon to stay with the children and let the wife take the car and do what she pleases. Maybe Saturday afternoon would not be best for every pastor, but certainly an afternoon could be worked out where the wife could be away from the children for awhile and enjoy the privacy of having the car alone.

7. Intensify the Schedule as the Week Progresses

The pastor should be constantly building toward the climax on Sunday. Hence, it is a good idea to intensify the schedule as the week progresses. In other words, take care of light matters such as personal business, church business, etc., in the early part of the week and gradually build up to a spiritual climax for Sunday. My soul-winning days are at the last of the week. The last of the week should be directed away from business matters. It is always a good idea to start the week with the light, less spiritual matters and gradually build toward a great climactic experience on Sunday.

8. A Suggested Weekly Schedule

Now let us look at the possible schedule for the pastor. This schedule is one that I have tried to follow through the years. Of course, speaking engagements have not always permitted and I have not always been as diligent as perhaps I should have been. But I suggest this type of schedule for every pastor.

Monday: Sleep late and get home early. A light day on Monday with perhaps office hours from 9 to 4; taking care of business, counseling, shut-in and hospital visits, etc. Monday is a good day to come home early and take the family out to eat in the evening.

Tuesday morning: business, counseling, letters, etc.

Tuesday afternoon: spend this time with the children.

Wednesday morning: business, counseling, letters, etc.

Wednesday afternoon: study.

Thursday morning: plan church visitation for Thursday evening. Also, other miscellaneous duties as the time permits.

Thursday afternoon: soul-winning visitation.

Friday morning: plan for the services on Sunday, study and other miscellaneous office tasks.

Friday afternoon: soul-winning visitation.

Saturday morning: work around the house such as mowing yard, repairing items until about eleven o'clock. A good time to visit is between eleven and one on Saturday.

Saturday afternoon: baby-sit for the wife while she goes to the store and has some time alone.

Saturday night: prayer and meditation and preparation of the heart for Sunday. Bear in mind, the preparation of the mind should have already been made. Spend some time preparing the heart for Sunday.

Sunday: public services, of course, with rest, study, and meditation in the afternoon.

This schedule may not fit your own need. The purpose of this article is not to suggest a schedule as much as it is to suggest having a schedule. Once again, the pastor who gets a lot done will do it on purpose. He will plan his life, plan his schedule, take advantage of every possible moment; keep his mind busy all the time. "Redeeming the time, because the days are evil."

May God help us to be God's men doing God's work in a systematically planned and spiritual way.

11
Let's Include the Family

So many preachers seem to have the idea that they must choose between the family and the work. This is not so. The truth of the matter is, the family is a part of the work. No preacher can be a good Christian unless he is a good father, a good husband and a good citizen.

The preacher who has a successful family life will do it on purpose and not accidentally. He must work and plan to have the proper relationship with his family. Many preachers' wives sacrifice what is rightfully theirs because preachers seem to think they must choose between being good evangelistic pastors and good husbands and fathers. Many children of evangelistic pastors do not receive what is rightfully theirs because of the same reason.

1. The Good Pastor Should Have a Happy Home

The pastor's evangelistic responsibilities and his family responsibilities supplement each other. Having a successful, happy family life will increase his evangelistic burden and make the pastor more successful in every phase of his work. No family should be more closely knit than the pastor's family. There are several reasons for this:

Because of the pastor himself. In many cases, the loneliest person in the church is the pastor. Due to his responsibilities to all, often he has few intimate friends. Because of the fear of showing partiality, the pastor oftentimes leans away from any close personal ties. This should drive him to his family. Because of this situation, the pastor should solidify his family relationships and find a closeness with his family that perhaps none of his members would find with their families.

Because of his wife. Oftentimes the pastor's wife is the loneliest woman in the church. Criticism and experience may have led her away from having close personal friends as other ladies enjoy. Because of this, she, too, needs the blessedness of a happy, closely-knit home. Brethren, let's not forget our wives. The pastor should not forget his wife nor leave her out of his schedule.

Because of the children. Whether we like it or not, our children live in a glass house. Whether we believe it or not, our children are considered at school and at play somewhat different from other children. This is especially true when the pastor has strong convictions and does not allow his child to participate in school dances and other social functions that would be considered wrong by spiritual people. The pastor's child is often criticized at school. He is often laughed at and made fun of. Often he is excluded from social functions by the convictions of his parents, his own convictions, or by the students themselves. Once again he must turn to his family. He must find fun, pleasure, warmth, and love at home. The place that is left vacant at school and at play and in his social life must be filled by a warm, close, family tie at home.

Because of example. The Bible preacher must, of course, preach on the home. He must lead his people to have close home ties and a happy home life. The best way to do this is by example. We must live what we preach in our home life as well as in our personal life.

2.   The Pastor and His Wife

The evangelistic pastor should definitely schedule time for his wife. He should make definite plans to be the proper kind of husband and to see that his wife is not overlooked in his busy schedule. There are several things he may do to help in this matter:

The pastor and his wife should stay in love. Preachers and and their wives can be sweethearts too. There is nothing wrong with the people of the church being aware of this situation. It is wholesome for the children to know that mother and father are in love with each other. Far too many of our young people think that handholding, kissing, and so forth is for the unmarried. The truth is just the opposite. It is for the married. Happy is the pastor who stays in love with his wife, and happy is the pastor's wife who has a sweetheart for a husband and pastor.

The pastor and his wife should spend time alone together. By very careful planning, the use of babysitters, careful budgeting of money and time, the pastor and his wife may spend many happy hours together. We have found it profitable in our home for Mrs. Hyles and me to visit together often. We perhaps will take the entire day, secure a babysitter, visit shut-ins and sick people in the morning, eat lunch together, then visit prospects in the afternoon. Often we find we need to get to know each other better, and it is refreshing to spend some time alone, just the two of us.

The pastor and his wife should win souls together. The preacher should not confine his spiritual activity to his preacher brethren and his members. Soul winning should be a part of his home as well as his ministry. Many homes would be happier if the husband and wife won souls together. Often Mrs. Hyles and I go visiting in the afternoon and see people saved. We have had many walk the aisle whom we won to Christ together in the homes.

We preachers should realize that if our wives are to stay spiritual and keep up with us in spiritual growth, we must include them in our spiritual activities. Many times a pastor comes to me complaining about the lack of spirituality manifested in his wife. Upon careful questioning, I find that he has never asked her to go soul winning with him, they have never visited together or won souls together. She has been tied up in the house with the children, with no outside spiritual interest or activity, thereby not having the opportunity for spiritual growth that her husband has had. This is tragic and sometimes leads to shipwreck in the home.

See that the pastor's wife has time alone. The busy pastor spends many hours in his study. This is as it should be. We must have time alone with God and His Book in order to know Him and the Book better. But how about the wife? Should not she, too, have time alone? Should not she, too, have some time to spend with God? Should not she, too, have some time to read the Book? I have found it convenient to baby-sit for my wife while she goes out for awhile. In the afternoon, when the children are at school and the babies are asleep, I can study just as well at home as I can at church. I can have privacy as I study at home and give the wife the car key and a few dollars and let her be by herself for awhile. At least half a day a week in this endeavor would brighten the life of many a pastor's wife and would enrich the home life of many a parsonage.

See that the wife spends some time with the children. By this, I mean time spent outside the house. The pastor's wife should become a pal with the children just as she must feed, clothe, and bathe them. This can only be possible when the pastor helps and encourages her in the planning of such outside activities.

Have regular appointments with the wife. Mrs. Hyles and I frequently have an appointment to eat together or to go somewhere together. For example, we often attend such things as flower shows, clean amusements, and so forth, with each other. When such a date is planned, I have an appointment with her just as I would have an appointment with someone else. If others want that time, I simply explain that I have a previous appointment. Should not our appointments with the family be kept as rigidly as those with the church members? What a shame to give the wife the left over time — if there is any — and there usually is none.

Be her pastor. This is one of the most difficult things about the ministry. The pastor's wife has just as much right to have a pastor as anyone else. Hence, she must have confidence in her husband. There must be times when she can talk with him about her problems and burdens. He should be as willing to advise her as he is to advise others. She should be able to retain her confidence in him, in order to have a pastor when one is needed. Of course this will necessitate being as good a Christian at home as you are at church, and being as good a Christian around your wife as you are around the wives of members. The pastor's wife should not have to sacrifice the right to have a pastor.

The pastor should not expect his wife to be his assistant pastor. Many a frustrated pastor's wife has thrown up her hands in failure and despair because she was unable to be all that she was expected to be. The pastor can remedy this situation with proper handling of the people and his wife. When the pulpit committee first contacts the pastor, the pastor should make it clear that his wife is the pastor's wife and not the assistant pastor. He should make it clear that being a soloist, pianist, organist, visitation director, and so forth, are not necessary qualifications of being a successful pastor's wife. It is more important that she be a successful wife to the pastor than a successful assistant. She should be considered as just another good Christian in the church. Her duties would be the same duties that any other good Christian wife would perform.

The pastor should protect the wife's privacy. Far too many parsonages are akin to Grand Central Station. Far too many pastors' homes are busier than Times Square. Often members take advantage of the pastor's home to make it their lounging place during an off-day, their stopping place during a ten-minute break, and the gossip center for all recent news. This can be avoided if the pastor will protect his wife's privacy. Why not use the study for conferences instead of the living room? When someone calls for a conference, why not meet them at the church? To be sure, the pastor's home should be open to guests, and the pastor and his wife should welcome guests, as any other family should. But this can be abused to the extent that the poor preacher's wife knows nothing of privacy in the home. The pastor may prevent this by doing his work at the office, his counseling at church, and planning the schedule of his family so there will not be enough idle time for such things as mentioned above.

The pastor and his wife should eat out alone once a week. This does not mean a sirloin steak necessarily. It could mean a 15-cent hamburger and a milkshake. Personally, I yearn for fellowship with my wife and for time to talk together. This can be done during one meal a week — eating anything from a hot dog and a soft drink to a thick steak in an elite restaurant.

The pastor should help his wife around the house. It has been my policy for many years to wash the dishes and clean up the kitchen on Sunday morning while the wife dresses the family for church. When the wife is exceptionally busy, the pastor could wash the dishes some evening for her. We must watch out that this does not become a daily routine and ritual, but it would be nice as an occasional gesture. God help us pastors and wives to like each other, to love each other, and to know each other.

3.   The Pastor and His Children

In reading the biographies of scores of great preachers and knowing literally hundreds of preachers personally, I have noticed that many preachers' children do not turn out right. Much of this could be avoided. As the writer of old said, "They made me the keeper of the vineyard; but my own vineyard have I not kept." The pastor should see to it that he is a good father and that his children do not have to sacrifice a father on the altar of being the preacher's kids. Following are suggestions for the pastor and his children.

Be expressive in love. Children should be taught to love their father and mother and to be expressive in such love. Such things as kissing good-by, kissing good night, and expressions like, "I love you, Daddy," and "I love you, Johnny," should be in the pastor's schedule. Through the years I have found it very advisable to take each child alone periodically and make love to the child. Tell him that you are proud to be his father and proud that he is your son. Tell him how you thank God for giving him to you and how you pray for God to use him in the future. Such moments are tender and precious and will certainly make richer the life of the child.

Many times young people come to me and say, "Brother Hyles, I feel I can talk to you, but I cannot talk to my parents." This would not be true if the parents spent some sweet hours during the child's life in expression of love and building of confidence.

The pastor should be pals with the children. Every week the pastor should include in his schedule some time with the children. Trips to the zoo, the park, a vacant-lot ball game, and other activities, would certainly endear the pastor to his children, and vice versa. One dollar invested in an amusement park where the children can ride the Ferris wheel or the merry-go-round would be a dollar invested in the life of the child. My daughters and I have through the years had occasional dates. I will take them out to eat or take them for a sandwich. I open the car door for them, help them out of the car, help them be seated at the restaurant, talk to them about their problems, help them back in the car, and act like we are on a date. This has been a thrilling experience through the years for me and for the children.

Not only should some time be spent with the children, but some time should be spent alone with each child. Each child should feel that he has a special place in his father's life and heart. There is a certain security that the only child in a family feels, that children in larger families do not feel. This security could be felt if periodically each child was the only child for an hour or so.

Pray daily for each child. Oh, how our children's lives should be bathed in our prayers! How we should take their names before the throne of grace every day, asking God to bless them and use them and make them what He wants them to be. Also, we should pray with the child. When my oldest girl was five or six years old, she had her first tooth to be pulled. I tried to pull it but could not. Frankly, I was a little nauseated and chickenhearted. I told her that it was not ready. She said, "Daddy, let's pray and ask Jesus to help us pull it." We bowed our heads, asked Jesus to help us pull the tooth, and, believe it or not, it came out the next jerk!

The pastor should train his children. This is especially true in the case of the son. Spending periodic times in teaching the child how to shake hands, look someone in the eye when they talk, behave in public and other things, would certainly reap dividends in the future. This could be done a few minutes before supper. It could be done on the way to church sometime. It could be done in the evening before going to bed.

The pastor should win souls with his children. This is one of the most precious things of my life. Periodically I take my children who are old enough soul winning with me. We have had some blessed experiences. Becky (who is now ten) and I have won many people together. One day we won a lady to Christ. Shortly after, the lady came to church, brought her ten-year-old daughter, and Becky won the daughter to

Christ. A few weeks later the father was saved, and now the family is happy in the Lord. One day recently Becky and I had the joy of leading three to Christ in an afternoon. She has learned to be a soul winner, and just two days ago was telling me that in the last three months she herself had won eleven people to Christ.

One day she called me over and said one of her friends was ready to be saved and she wanted me to talk to her friend. I said to her in the presence of her friend, "What did you call me for? You have taken the soul winning course. You have seen me win scores of people. You win her." I sat there with the children as Becky went through the plan of salvation, the Roman Road. She led the child to pray, prayed herself, then lead the child to Christ. I questioned the child very carefully and was assured the child had real conversion. She told her mother, her mother was convinced the child was saved, and the child was baptized the next Sunday night.

Again I say, do not keep your soul-winning blessings away from the family.

The pastor should teach his children. Do not leave all of the teaching up to the Sunday School teachers and superintendents and what you teach in the pulpit. The pastor should teach the Bible to his children. The way we do this most effectively is by having the children outline my sermons on Sunday. My boy David, who is now eight, has a big stack of sermon outlines he keeps. He outlines every sermon I preach.

Going home from church, at home from church, or sometime during the week, we review the sermon, high points, the story involved, and instruct the children as to the teachings in the sermon that they should understand. May God help us as preachers and evangelistic pastors to be good fathers, rearing our children in the nurture and admonition of the Lord.

4. The Pastor's Wife and the Pastor's Children

As mentioned previously, the pastor's wife should take time with the children. This is one of the most 'difficult things in the life of a busy pastor. It must be planned and carefully adhered to. Let us notice some suggestions about this matter.

The pastor's wife and children should not have lives filled with drudgery. The pastor's wife should have fun with the children. She, too, should spend time alone with them. Mrs. Hyles often takes the children with her window-shopping, out to eat, grocery-shopping, or to buy necessary clothes for them. Each of these occasions should be planned and made into a big event. Someone has said that the mother is the one the child wants when in need and the father is the pal the child wants when wanting to play. This should not be so and would not be so if the mother would take time with the children for entertainment and fellowship outside the house.

The mother should train and teach the children. Due to the many and varied activities of the pastorate, much of the training and teaching of the children will be left to the pastor's wife. The best example I know of is Susannah Wesley. Even though she was the mother of nineteen children, she took time each week for each child alone. For example, every Thursday night John Wesley spent some time alone with his mother. She taught him manners, graces, habits, and other things a young man should know. My, what dividends were reaped in the lives of John and Charles Wesley! Great dividends could be reaped in your home and mine, too.

The pastor's wife should discipline herself and her schedule to include the children. No doubt the hardest life in the family to discipline is that of the mother. Hence, it is best to have a definite time and a definite day. The father can baby-sit or let the wife have the car and a few dollars to spend with her children.

5. The Entire Family

Togetherness should be the word for the pastor's family. There are many things that can be done together and should be done together to bind tighter the unity of the family.

Meals should be eaten together. The pastor and his family should definitely enjoy times of fellowship around the table. This is scriptural and right. How sad it is when different members of the family eat at different times of the day. For many years now, we have taken time in the morning for a good breakfast together. This starts the day off with the family circle complete. We can discuss the day's activities and have a little fun together around the table.

The family may spend the evenings together. I work my schedule so as to have a certain amount of evenings to spend with the family. When I schedule an evening with the family, it is just as much a scheduled day as if I had a speaking engagement. Oh, if the pastor would just give his family the same privileges he gives others.

Good games can be played together. There are many good, clean games that can be purchased for next to nothing and can be enjoyed by the entire family. Occasionally we make it a point to purchase a new game that the family can play together. Of course, the pastor must be very careful not to win too much, lest he break up a happy home!

The family should go to church together. We have made it a habit through the years to try to go to church together. In other words, not one at one time and another at another time, but all of us as a family unit preparing for church together, helping to dress the little ones and getting off to an early start to enjoy the trip to church. These can be precious moments.

The family should eat out together. About once a week,

it is always good for the entire family to go out to some restaurant to eat. This should be announced early so that the children can look forward to it. This is always a refreshing, delightful time. Take a couple of hours for it. Do not be in a hurry. Sit around the table, eat slowly and have a big time. It can be a real help in solidifying family life.

The family should take a vacation together. We look forward every year to vacationtime. We plan a real active vacation, with a real good time for everybody. Start early in planning the vacation. Remind the children about the number of days until vacationtime. One of the best ways in the world to keep a happy family is to look forward to events together. With proper planning and promotion, the family can have wonderful times daily looking forward to events such as the vacation.

The family should play together. There are many family amusements that can be done within the convictions of the average pastor. There should definitely be time scheduled in the pastor's life where the family can have some amusement time together. I have always hoped that my children would make their home the center of their amusement life. If the pastor and his wife plan properly, the children can have more fun at home and with the family than they can with others. The reason many of our children today go away from home for their fun is that there is so little fun at home. The reason they want to spend more time apart from the family is that they have more fun apart from the family. May God help us to direct and plan our children's lives so the family can play together.

There should be the family altar time. Perhaps the one family in the church that finds it hardest to have a family altar is the pastor's family. The schedule is interrupted so much and there are so many different activities separating the family members. We have found it best to have our family altar in the evening. We have four children. We all get on one of the beds in the house, sit up and listen to the reading of the Bible. Due to the age of our children, we do not have a lengthy Bible reading. We take turns in reading — one night I will read, one night Mrs. Hyles will read, one night Becky will read, and occasionally our eight-year-old David will read. After that we ask a question or two about the Bible reading. We memorize one verse a week and go over it each evening. Then we kneel around the bed and pray one at a time. Cindy, who is two, usually must be told what to pray. Linda, who is four; David, who is eight; and Becky, who is ten, say their own prayers. Then Mrs. Hyles prays and I close.

The family altar time is never camp-meeting style. It never reminds one of a Billy Sunday revival. But it is a time when each one in our family hears each other one in the family call his name in prayer. This should be done in all homes and especially in the pastor's home.

The Bible has the answer to every problem. May God help the pastor to have a Bible home so he can help in solving the problems of those who have home difficulties within his church. May God use these few suggestions to make our home and yours what it ought to be.

12
Let's Conserve the Results

A real active soul-winning church loses more converts than any other kind of church. The reason is that such a church *makes* more converts; hence, more converts are kept and more converts are lost.

Much care should be taken with every convert to be sure that nothing has been spared to conserve him and make him a useful and useable Christian in the service of the Lord.

One of the criticisms levied against soul-winning churches often is that they "dip 'em and drap 'em." We should do all that we can to make this criticism an unjustified one. In John 15, verse 16, we are told "that your fruit should remain." We are told in Matthew 28:19 and 20 to "teach them to observe all things whatsoever I have commanded you." These and other Scriptures would lead us to believe that much effort should be given to conserve the results of our evangelistic program. In this chapter we plan to take a step-by-step observation of the follow-up work done in our church. May God use it to help others.

1. Someone Prays With the New Convert at the Altar
This is covered carefully in the chapter on giving an invitation. We feel that when a person is properly dealt with at

the altar, it is the first step in an effective follow-up program.

We have thirty-three deacons in our church. Each of these men is instructed concerning dealing with people at the altar. When a person comes to be saved, one of our deacons kneels at the altar with the new convert, opens the Bible, prays with him, and leads him to assurance of salvation.

2. The Convert Then Has a Seat on the Front, Where the Secretary Makes a Record of His Conversion

This record is made in triplicate form. One copy is given to the pastor to read to the people. Another copy is given to the assistant pastor for follow-up work. The third copy is used in our church records. Below is a copy of the form we use.

Name_____ Date_____

Address_____ Apt._____

City_____ Age_____

Decision:

        ☐ PROFESSION OF FAITH
        ☐ BAPTISM
        ☐ TRANSFER
        ☐ CHRISTIAN EXPERIENCE
        ☐ RESTORATION

Present Membership:

        Church_____

        City_____

---

3. The Pastor Reads the Convert's Name to the People

The person stands at the front and pastor, people, and convert rejoice a moment over his salvation. At this time friends or members of the family come forward to stand with him to rejoice about the victory. This is also covered in the chapter on giving an invitation.

4. The People Come By to Shake the Convert's Hand

This is a time of definite follow-up work. The people come and rejoice with the convert over his decision. This gives him more assurance and confidence in his experience.

5. The Secretary Gives Him a Letter About Baptism

The church secretary comes by to shake hands with the converts. She has a mimeographed letter from the pastor for each convert. The letter explains the meaning of baptism, the things to bring to baptism, and the time and place to meet. This letter is given to the converts at the altar as the secretary shakes their hands.

6. The Assistant Pastor Talks With Each About Baptism

As the assistant pastor goes down the line, he talks with each person about the necessity of being baptized and following Christ in baptism and church membership. He also informs them as to the time and place of the meeting for baptism. Actually, he simply gives a vocal encouragement to the written one previously given by the secretary. At this time, the assistant pastor tries to get a verbal commitment from them to come and get baptized that night.

7. A Letter Is Sent to Each Convert the Following Tuesday

On Tuesday a personal letter goes from the pastor to each convert rejoicing with him over his decision. This letter is not mimeographed, but typewritten, and is signed by the pastor.

8. A Baptism Letter Goes Out During the Following Week

Those who are saved on Sunday, but chose not to be baptized then, receive a letter about baptism, encouraging them to come the next Sunday night for baptism. This letter is sent out each week for four weeks in an effort to get them baptized.

9. There Is a Baptism Class Each Sunday at 6:30 in the Evening

In our church we baptize every Sunday evening following the evening service. This has been our policy for over ten years now. Only two Sunday nights in the last ten years have we not baptized. In our present pastorate we have found it advisable to have a baptism class before baptism. The class meets at 6:30 each Sunday evening. The assistant pastor teaches it. For a number of years the pastor taught it and occasionally still does.

At this class several things are discussed. First, and most important, is the meaning of baptism. The convert is taught that baptism pictures the death, burial, and resurrection of Christ; that it pictures our death to sin and rising again to walk in newness of life; that it pictures our identification with Christ in His death; and that it is a public declaration of an inward experience.

At this meeting the mode of baptism is discussed. In other words, the person is shown exactly how he is to be baptized.

This eliminates a number of fears, especially for little children, and prepares them to know exactly what will happen when they are baptized.

After the meeting the people are taken to the dressing room, where they leave their extra clothes. They are asked to sit in a group in the auditorium.

We might note also that we use baptismal robes or smocks. They are very simple garments made of white cotton material, and make a very impressive baptismal scene. Oftentimes someone who is converted on Sunday night can be baptized immediately because of this arrangement.

10. The Convert Receives a Visit From the Pastor the Following Week

This may be done by the pastor or the assistant pastor or another staff member. The purpose of this visit is:

(1) to check the experience of salvation very carefully;

(2) to discuss baptism and church membership with the convert;

(3) to enroll the family in Sunday School if at all possible;

(4) to acquaint them with our church life and the opportunities our church affords;

(5) to witness to other members of the family who might be unsaved.

11. Have a New Member's Reception Each Month

Once each month our church has what we call a New Members' Reception. This reception is a special meeting attended by the new members in the church and the church officers, such as staff, deacons, etc. The purpose of this meeting is to acquaint the new member with our church life and introduce him to our church leaders.

The meeting is begun with a song. This song can have something to do with growth in grace or another timely subject. Then the pastor welcomes the new members on behalf of the church. The pastor asks the deacons to stand, and then one at a time the church officers are introduced as follows: pastor, assistant pastor, music and youth director, secretaries, chairman of the deacons, deacons, church treasurer, W. M. S. president, etc.

After a word of greeting from the pastor, the assistant pastor is called on. He also gives a word of greeting and explains a few things about the church program. Then the music and youth director takes five minutes to introduce them to the youth program of the church and also the music program. He also adds his word of greeting.

Then the rest of the staff and deacons are introduced. The deacon chairman is called upon, and he speaks a word of welcome to the new members. The W. M. S. president is presented. She tells about the ladies' missionary work of the church and invites all the ladies to participate in this activity.

After the different leaders of the church have been introduced, some slides are shown to acquaint the new member with the different activities of the church. First, we show them pictures of the offices and buildings. Included in these buildings are the pastor's home, the assistant pastor's home, the branch churches, the custodian's home, etc. Then we show some pictures about growing in grace.

We show a slide of a family having a family altar. Another slide is shown of a person knocking on a door, going visiting. Another slide is shown of a family at the table with heads bowed thanking God for the food. Other slides concerning growth in grace are shown, as we encourage the new converts and new members to include these suggestions in their life. Then we show slides of our mission work. As the slides are shown someone explains the different phases of the church program. Pictures of our missionaries are shown to the people. Pictures of other phases of our church life are shown. The financial program of the church is shown. In other words, slides concerning every phase of our church life are given to acquaint them quickly with their new church.

After these slides have been shown, there is a prayer of dedication and consecration by the pastor for the members, thanking God for them and asking His blessings upon our new relationship together.

Also at this meeting there is presented to the new member a packet for new members. In this packet there is a book of daily devotional thoughts to help in their private devotions. There is a copy of the church covenant. There is a copy of the church constitution article concerning membership. There is a book of instruction for new Christians. There is a certificate of church membership. There is also a packet of envelopes for the year. This packet is given to every new member to help them in their spiritual growth.

Following the presentation of the packet, there is a time of refreshment and fellowship. The new members go by a table, get some punch and cookies, and have a seat. The deacons and leaders in the church also get refreshments and are instructed to mix and mingle with the new people, meeting each of them and welcoming them into the fellowship of our church.

This is a very profitable time, and goes a long way to make new members feel welcome in the church.

12.   Have a Three-Week Class for New Members

At the New Members' Reception, announcement is made concerning a class for new members. This class is taught the three Sunday evenings following the New Members' Reception — from 5:45 to 6:30. The courses taught are as follows: soul winning, fundamental Bible truths, habits for new Christians, how to work for the Lord, etc.

The last Sunday evening a tour is made of the church property, showing the people the different departments, the offices, the church library, book store, the nurseries, and other interesting places on the church property.

13. The Sunday School Teachers Visit Them Every Time They Are Absent

The best follow-up work is the Sunday School. When a person is voted into our church, we enroll him in Sunday School, and then when he is absent he is visited by his teacher. This should be done constantly and consistently. Our motto is: Absentees are people. Our constant reminder is the most important absentee to visit is the one who was absent last Sunday for the first time. Chronic absentees are made of such people. We insist that our teachers visit the one who was absent the first time the last Sunday before other visits. He is the one who can be gotten back and must be reclaimed quickly.

You can see by the above program that a new member of our church receives a maximum of six letters, one visit, five classes of instruction, six weeks of interest, and over six hours of personal attention. To be sure, we still lose many. But we feel when the criticism comes that we "dip 'em and drap 'em," it is unjustified, for we have done our best to teach them "all things whatsoever I have commanded you" and 'that our fruit should remain.'